Integrating Psychology, Religion, and Culture

Religion and Psychology

Volumes published in the Brill Research Perspectives title are listed at *brill.com/rpsy*

Integrating Psychology, Religion, and Culture

The Promise of Qualitative Inquiry

By

Jenny H. Pak

BRILL

LEIDEN | BOSTON

This paperback book edition is simultaneously published as issue 2.4 (2020) of *Religion and Psychology*, DOI:10.1163/25897128-12340006.

Library of Congress Control Number: 2020922353

Typeface for the Latin, Greek, and Cyrillic scripts: "Brill". See and download: brill.com/brill-typeface.

ISBN 978-90-04-44961-9 (paperback)
ISBN 978-90-04-44964-0 (e-book)

This book is printed on acid-free paper and produced in a sustainable manner.

Contents

Integrating Psychology, Religion, and Culture

The Promise of Qualitative Inquiry

Jenny H. Pak
Fuller Graduate School of Psychology, Pasadena, California, USA
jpak@fuller.edu

Abstract

Although science was originally broadly conceptualized as a systematic, rigorous activity to produce trustworthy knowledge, psychologists, those following the mainstream, adopted a single philosophy of science and strictly enforced natural science as the only proper "scientific" psychology. Qualitative research has been part of modern psychology from the beginning, but it was obscured for nearly a century as positivist epistemology came to dominate the field. Building culturally robust and intelligible theories capable of responding more effectively to complex problems faced by a rapidly changing world calls for openness in methodological diversity. Deeply rooted in a hermeneutic tradition, cultural psychology has challenged the appropriateness of seeking reductive knowledge because higher mental processes such as religious beliefs, values, and choices are bound by historical and cultural context. As greater interdisciplinary integration and methodological innovations are necessary to keep psychology of religion relevant, narrative inquiry has emerged as a promising integrative paradigm.

Keywords

cultural psychology – psychology of religion – qualitative methodology – narrative inquiry

1 Introduction: History of Qualitative Inquiry, Psychology and Religion

In order to get a sense of qualitative psychology and to assess what its potential contributions to the future of psychology of religion might be, it is essential to understand its history. Experts credit Wundt for not only the founding of

 | DOI:10.1163/9789004449640_002

modern psychology in 1879 with the creation of the first psychological experimental laboratory in Leipzig, but also the establishment of *Völkerpsychologie* (folk or cultural psychology) grounded in qualitative research (Danziger, 1983; Leahey, 2000). Major works by Wundt and others such as James, Watson, Binet, Freud, Piaget, Kohlberg, and Maslow were inspired by qualitative investigation, but the value of the methods they employed were hidden until more recently (Giorgi, 2009; Stainton Rogers & Willig, 2017; Wertz et al., 2011). In critically examining well-known experimental studies in social psychology, Stainton Rogers (2011) observed:

> What *appear* to be simple social psychological experiments are often not all that simple or even that experimental. Researchers either deliberately or serendipitously get other data [qualitative] than the bald numbers of the measures they have reported and, I suspect, often use this data to help them understand what is going on either overtly or covertly. What is interesting, though, is that this very important qualitative component and the abductive logic it stimulates are not so much covered up as ignored by social psychology textbooks… The consequence is that we are left with a sense that experimental work is all about the numbers, when, I suspect, it is seldom so clear-cut. (pp. 111–112)

In this way, the value of information beyond numbers was used unsystematically and remained unacknowledged.

Although qualitative inquiry has been part of modern psychology from its very beginning, quantitative research came to control the field with generalization and measurement, denouncing any other method unscientific (Leary, 2014; Stainton Rogers & Willig, 2017; Wertz, 2014). In the late nineteenth and early twentieth centuries, with the 'physics envy,' psychologists adopted the single philosophy of science view, which strictly enforced 'scientific psychology' as natural science (Cole, 1996; Leahey, 2000; Polkinghorne, 1983; Riegel, 1976; Stainton Rogers & Willig, 2017). Following the positivist notion that the nature of reality is grounded in empirical observations, psychology reinforced three major assumptions: (1) the stability of behavior and relationships over time and space, (2) universal applicability, and (3) objectivity. Mentalism and consciousness as the subject matter of psychology was replaced by behaviorism and restricted to objective measure; as the discipline reconfigured, qualitative research was obscured for over a century (Danziger, 1990).

Scholars challenged the appropriateness of seeking universally true knowledge pointing out that psychological theory, unlike physics, is bound by historical and cultural context; it has been also explicated that reductionist materialism which may have been successful in the physical and biological realm breaks down when it comes to the higher mental processes such as beliefs, values, and choices (Gergen, 1973; Polkinghorne, 1983; Riegel, 1975, 1976; Taylor, 1992). For over a century, Continental philosophers have argued that the subject matter of psychology requires embracing methodology appropriate for human subjects, but psychologists persisted in relying exclusively on natural science methods and marginalizing qualitative approaches (Polkinghorne, 1983; Wertz, 2011). Scientism, the dogmatic belief in natural science as the only valid way to do science (Bannister, 1987; Davis, 2009), took over psychology more than any other discipline as it "sought public esteem as a 'science' by displaying signals of rigorous control, expert detachment, and reduction of the objects of study to numerical representations of reality" (Thin, 2018, p. 1). Taylor (1992) articulates "the great fault of modern psychology is that it is entirely too quantitative… the fetish for numbers, which justifies psychology as a science" (p. 293).

The dominance of natural science as the only 'proper psychology' had devastating consequences for human science and the qualitative research tradition (Stainton Rogers & Willig, 2017). In a brief historical overview of qualitative inquiry in psychology, Wertz (2014) notes that qualitative methodology received little or no attention in psychology until Gordon Allport was commissioned by the Social Science Research Council in 1940; however, even after Allport (1942) documented the importance of idiographic approaches in generating theory and scientific knowledge, psychology continued to lag behind other disciplines (e.g., anthropology, sociology, education, women's studies, medicine, nursing, social work). It took another 30 years before qualitative research gained receptivity in psychology because of strict adherence to hypothesis testing, measurement, and statistics despite numerous warnings about their misuse (e.g., Cumming et al., 2007; Lamiell, 1981, 2019; Porter, 1995; Scheff, 2011; Ziliak & McCloskey, 2008).

Even though the philosophical assumptions of science have been scrutinized for many years, Wertz (2011) indicates that it was primarily the emancipatory movements of the 1960s, which gave a platform to the previously oppressed such as women (e.g., Gilligan, 1982) and other groups (e.g., low SES, racial/ethnic minorities, third- and fourth-world peoples), that prompted the academic circles to shift, created space for methodological diversity, and, ultimately, allowed qualitative research to emerge in psychology. As the hegemony of dominant ideologies was dismantled, a broadening concept of science engendered researchers to find a new "ethically grounded epistemology" that empowered diverse groups that had been traditionally neglected (Wertz, 2011). Following Europe, Australia, New Zealand, and Canada's lead, the United States eventually became open to qualitative methods that were more responsive and empathic to participants' experience and engagement in the research process (Marecek, Fine, & Kidder, 1997). Subsequently, since the 1990s, qualitative studies have begun to appear more regularly in psychological journals (Rennie, Watson, & Monteiro, 2002).

The increasing traction of social movements for democratization, liberation, and justice around the world has fostered an explosive growth of qualitative research and radically transformed the social sciences over the last three decades; this shift has been called the "qualitative revolution" (Denzin & Lincoln, 2000; Wertz, 2011). This movement was also fueled by a 'turn to language' as well as a 'turn to interpretation' in social science epistemology, which allowed researchers to deconstruct psychological knowledge construction and qualitative research to be more widely acceptable (Stainton Rogers & Willig, 2017). These shifts eventuated in establishing a distinct branch of psychology through the emergence of the Society for Qualitative Inquiry in Psychology (SQIP), which later merged with Division 5 (formerly the Division of Evaluation, Measurement, and Statistics; now the Division of Quantitative and Qualitative Methods) in the American Psychological Association in 2013. As the editor of the divisional journal, *Qualitative Psychology*, Josselson (2014) states in the inaugural issue that it was birthed with a commitment to a vision of broadening investigation that focuses on understanding the human experience holistically and contextually from the point of view of the acting subject. She further elaborates the mission of the journal:

> In taking its place in the pantheon of psychological study, qualitative inquiry is rejoining the integrative ideas of psychology's founders, reclaiming directions laid out by William James and Wilhelm Wundt (among others)... It is not new, but it got sidelined as psychology pursued other directions in the 20th century. We envision this journal as being a home for qualitative inquiry—a place for qualitative researchers to gather as they map out this reclaimed path to a different kind of psychological understanding, a science based more in hermeneutics than positivism, grounded in interpretation rather than statistical analysis... The focus is on the scientific explication of qualities of human experience rather than the mathematical measure of atomized aspects of it. The journal is a place to explore and to realize the promise of qualitative investigation. (p. 2)

2 The Human Sciences: A Call for Methodological Pluralism

Extending back to not only Wundt, but also scholars like Dilthey, for more than a century, the human sciences were established in the discipline to propose methodological reform for the appropriate study of human experience and action that is embodied, historical, and integral (Cole, 1996; Polkinghorne, 1988). The reformers stressed the difference between the natural and human realm and called for multiple systems of inquiry to supplement traditional research. The philosophy of science has changed radically over several decades as the old "objectivist" paradigm was challenged by a new constructivist paradigm that emphasizes: (1) there are no certain knowledge claims, (2) no single system of knowledge has cognitive privilege, and (3) diverse systems of inquiry or research paradigms can produce useful knowledge (Polkinghorne, 1983).

In his early essays in psychology, James (1878/1983) proposed "all human thinking is essentially of two kinds—reasoning on the one hand, and narrative, descriptive, contemplative thinking on the other" (p. 237). This idea was later taken up by Bruner (1986) who elaborated upon the differences between two modes of thought—paradigmatic mode exemplified by the logico-scientific model and narrative mode. *Paradigmatic mode* attempts to fulfill the ideal through a formal, mathematical system of description and explanation, and employs categorization; it seeks to explain the underlying relationships between sets of observable variables and offers the power of prediction in that it sets up and tests hypotheses about the nature of reality. *Narrative mode*, on the other hand, is concerned with the meaning that is ascribed to experiences through stories; it organizes the complex and often ambiguous world of human intention and action into a meaningful structure (Polkinghorne, 1988).

Although these two modes are complementary, they are not reducible to one another (O'Neill, 2002; Polkinghorne, 1988). Each way of knowing has operating principles of their own and their own criteria of well-formedness. They differ radically in their procedures for verification. As a result, the merits of paradigmatic arguments and narrative stories cannot be judged by the same criteria. While good paradigmatic explanations should accurately predict observable phenomena, good narratives should meaningfully capture the shifting contours of lived experience. An equal appreciation and incorporation of both serve as the indispensable foundation for an ethical practice. What does not get addressed in psychology, Polkinghorne argues, are the relative contributions of each mode and their fundamental irreducibility. He called attention to narrative rationality, which belongs uniquely to human sciences and involves the vicissitudes of human intentions and realms of meaning while natural science methods fail to capture the meaning of human action.

Recognizing the complex and historical character of human beings, this shift has led to a call for methodological diversity, which Polkinghorne (1983) explains is not necessarily to replace quantitative but to add qualitative research methods that utilize ordinary language systems to cover areas that can never be addressed by the traditional logical-mathematical system, such as: (1) the generation of categories for understanding human phenomena and (2) the investigation of the interpretation and meaning people give to their experiences. This does not mean one methodology is better or more sophisticated than the other but recognizes the unique contribution of each approach and the interdependence between them (Davis, 2009; O'Neill, 2002; Polkinghorne, 1983).

A complementary approach emphasizes a methodological pluralism, in which diverse research methods are viewed in a horizontal fashion rather than ordered vertically with experiment at the top and others ranked below (Davis, 2009). In a complementary model, the research questions determine the methodological choice: while some questions are appropriate for quantitative methods, qualitative is best if the questions involve understanding participants' experience and meaning in context. This will encourage not only a better balance between quantitative and qualitative publications in major journals, but also allow access to complex phenomena that are of special interest to researchers—for example, the areas of psychology, religion, and culture, which seek to integrate the full range of human experience. Thus, methodological pluralism rooted deeply in a broad philosophical base avoids the limitations of a narrow scientism with its exclusionary dependence on natural science methods and furthers the basic goals and values of science, which is critical to properly studying whole human behavior and experience (Davis, 2009; Josselson, 2014; Polkinghorne, 1983).

Due to a strong commitment to positivist epistemology and methodology, a tolerance for pluralism, ambiguity, and limitation in the quest for knowledge has traditionally not been well received in Western psychology developed primarily in North America and Europe (Belzen & Hood, 2006). In the structural framework of logical positivism and natural science methodology (e.g., experimental and quantitative research), deductive reasoning is valued for its precision and internal consistency; however, as Polkinghorne (1983) reminds us, this is one form of rationality through which human beings order and make sense of experience. The precision of deductive reasoning is often more problematic than helpful in most psychological investigations, such as those found in cultural psychology and religion, where complex, interrelated events with loose concepts require a deeper understanding of human meaning and choice (Pak, 2017).

The history of psychology and qualitative research show 'science' is a historical concept (Danziger, 1990; Leahey, 2000). Prior to the dominance of hypothetico-deductivism in recent history (e.g., beginning in the 1950s with Karl Popper), science was originally conceptualized much more broadly as "a systematic, rigorous, empirical endeavor" to produce trustworthy knowledge rather than focused rigidly on method; for this reason, all qualitative methods are "equally valid and empirical" as data is gathered and analyzed to interpret findings (Stainton Rogers & Willig, 2017, p. 7). Descriptions of "good science" is not accumulating facts but includes characteristics such as: creativity, curiosity, and openness to seeking new understanding; examining parts in relation to the larger whole; accepting ambiguity, humility, and patience throughout the process of inquiry; and acknowledging personal and cultural bias (Davis, 2009).

2.1 *Misuses of Mixed-Method*

As the polarization between quantitative and qualitative research paradigms has broken down and mixed-method research has become recognized as a 'budding new approach' in recent years (e.g., Davis et al. 2016), the conventional distinction drawn between these two approaches on the surface level (e.g., the use of numbers versus words) tends to gloss over fundamental philosophical divergence (Alvesson & Skoldberg, 2017; Marecek, 2011). Goertz and Mahoney (2012) suggest it is vital to recognize quantitative and qualitative research traditions as two distinct cultures with their own coherent system of values, norms, and practices. They stress qualitative approaches should not be used as a last resort when statistical analysis is not possible and only cross boundary with mixed-method research if investigators are pursuing goals consistent with both research paradigms. However, as mixed methods research has become increasingly popular in psychology, a qualitative approach is frequently used like a 'handmaiden' to serve quantitative research purposes (e.g., a useful exploratory step to developing hypotheses or constructing instruments) instead of properly apprehending contrasting strengths and distinct research goals (Goertz & Mahoney, 2012; Pak, 2017; Stainton-Rogers & Willig, 2017).

Mixed-method research is conceptually more complex than simply combining different data and procedures. In fact, Creswell and Plano Clark (2010) strongly recommend that it should only be considered after the researcher has obtained adequate experience and knowledge with quantitative and qualitative research separately. While mixed methods could potentially provide added rigor, they also create challenges of mixing different methodology and procedures with distinct underlying philosophical worldviews. They require understanding the different purpose, logic, and assumptions guiding both qualitative and quantitative research design before one plans a study. Tailoring the purpose of the inquiry to research designed to address the question is essential in order to meaningfully analyze and produce knowledge that integrates more complete understandings of phenomena within cultural and religious contexts (Pak, 2017).

2.2 *Big-Q/Small-Q Distinctions*

Alvesson and Skoldberg (2017) indicate what contributes to the confusion is that most qualitative methods similarly follow positivist assumptions (e.g., objectivity, generalizability, precision, rigor, verification). For example, one of the most popular qualitative methods, grounded theory falls under neo-positivism in that empirical evidence is heavily emphasized and theory and interpretations are treated as separate from data. One helpful way to navigate differences among qualitative approaches is the 'Big-Q/small-q' demarcation offered by Kidder and Fine (1987). The small-q refers to research in which the questions are set in the quantitative paradigm (e.g., the insertion of open-ended questions into a survey or experiment) and non-numerical data is simply incorporated into hypothetico-deductive designs using predetermined categories. On the other hand, in Big-Q research, open-ended, inductive methodologies are utilized (i.e., does not proceed with specific hypotheses, predetermined variables, or rigid data collection procedure) to generate theory and gain new insights through exploration of participants' lived experiences and meaning.

The purpose of qualitative inquiry is understanding not only diverse human experiences in cultural contexts, but also hard-to-define phenomena related to meaning, purpose, intentionality, and spirituality, and revealing their deep structure (Davis, 2009; Denzin & Lincoln, 2000; Josselson, 2014; Pak, 2017; Polkinghorne, 1983; Stainton Rogers & Willig, 2017; Thin, 2018). Most criticisms about qualitative research are frequently generated by misunderstanding the purpose of qualitative inquiry and judging qualitative studies using criteria derived from quantitative methodology. For example, based on positivist assumptions, large data collection may be valued, and qualitative studies are frequently criticized for small sample sizes (Pak, 2017). In order to avoid committing such an error, it is important to keep in mind that the goal of qualitative research is *not* generalization. Qualitative data does not offer the type of probabilistic, generalizable explanations that natural science inquiry seeks (Polkinghorne, 1983). In fact, it is critical to recognize that even quantitative research is not meant to apply to every individual in a given population but merely to capture trends. That is, no matter how robust a scientific finding about a given group, there will be exceptions that do not embrace the trend. Furthermore, the finding may not even apply to any individual in the group, as group level analysis does not apply to each individual.

Because 'pure data' or facts do not exist apart from interpretation, whether quantitative or qualitative, Alvesson and Skoldberg (2017) highlight that the most valuable aspects of research are interpretive and reflexive activities. Because method cannot be viewed independent from theory and other elements of preunderstanding (e.g., socio-political and cultural background, research community, language), researchers must actively engage in critical reflection. It is important to recognize that science is not divorced from culture, but a dialectical relationship exists between culture and research (Danziger, 1990; Kuhn, 1970). In fact, like yin and yang, they are inseparable and intimately connected to each other (Pak, 2017). Polkinghorne (1983) explains that knowledge is always perspectival and context-bound in that "apodictic knowledge is impossible, because human beings cannot stand outside their language systems and cultures and obtain an absolute viewpoint. All of our knowledge is conditional knowledge, constructed within our conceptual systems, and thus knowledge is a communal achievement and is relative to time and place" (p. 13).

Thus, culture shapes every aspect of knowledge formation and production, including what is considered valuable to research and how it is investigated. Dueck (1995) reminds researchers that we are not only the product of our culture, but also "ethical (moral) agents" of a particular culture in that we also *create* culture. The topics and the methods chosen, or not chosen, for a study may have implications not only for the academic discipline, but also society (e.g., an increasing push for evidence-based practice in medicine, mental health services, and education). While some may adapt more explicitly political perspectives and research methods to serve the purpose of empowering socially disadvantaged groups (e.g., critical theory, feminism, postcolonialism, community psychology), others who are agnostic about values may prefer to view research as having no purpose other than to increase general knowledge. Most psychologists are likely to be somewhere in between these two ends of the continuum (see Stainton Rogers & Willig, 2017 for a wide range of point of views and positions).

Interestingly, Alvesson and Karreman (2007) indicate that open and creative dialogues with empirical data actually serve as a source of inspiration or "mystery" in theory development by breaking down issues in existing theoretical frameworks. Thus, it is not 'objective' distancing of data but robust engagement with participants and context which permits investigators to gain a deeper understanding of particular phenomena (cf. Devereux, 1967). Increasingly, qualitative psychologists are engaging with research questions involving interpretation (Alvesson & Skoldberg, 2017; Josselson, 2014; Stainton Rogers & Willig, 2017). More specifically, investigators are asking questions about the cultural, religious, and psychological structures and processes and utilizing thick descriptions of qualitative data and analysis to explain phenomena, enrich understanding, and critically examine existing psychological theories (e.g., Belzen, 1999; Hood & Williamson, 2008; Kim & Pak 2013; Pak, 2006; Stainton Rogers & Willig, 2017). Although diverse qualitative research methods are growing in other parts of the world, Marecek (2011) observes American psychology continues to resist integrating the Big Q or interpretive approaches.

2.3 *Psychology, Religion, and Qualitative Inquiry*

In a historical overview, Parsons and Jonte-Pace (2001) map the interaction and debate between psychology and religion into three major periods: (1) "Psychology of religion" (1880–1930); (2) "Religion in dialogue with psychology" (1950–); and (3) "Psychology 'as' religion" (1970–). Although many attempts have been made to bring some cohesion to diverse dialogues and approaches (e.g., pastoral psychology, psychology and theology, psychology of religion, culture studies of religion), these authors question whether it can even be called a single field, but they prefer to use the broad designation "religion and psychological studies" (RPS) without privileging either term.

Of these three domains, Browning (2001) specifically locates 1950–1970s as the period the field of religion and psychological studies was officially "born and institutionalized" (p. 165). He strongly advocates the field of religion and psychological studies can best achieve its full potential through "critical hermeneutics." Based on Paul Ricoeur's work (1981), Browning suggests rather than "shallow empiricism," or positivistic emphasis on objectivity, "distanciation" in hermeneutic dialogue and understanding would be more useful in religio-cultural inquiry implicitly shared by theology, philosophy, and modern social sciences. Specifically, one promising area of integration he points out is using a critical theory of action informed by religion to serve as a background for addressing contemporary social problems. In this way, Browning views "a critical practical theology and a critical hermeneutics are nearly identical" (p. 176).

More recently scholars in this area have been differentiating the concept *spirituality* (i.e., relating to the sacred; Pargament, 2007) and *religion* (i.e., referring to the institutional context; Pargament, Mahoney, Exline, Jones, & Shafranske, 2013). As these constructs have been increasingly recognized as distinct, the APA Division 36 Psychology of Religion was renamed the Society for the Psychology of Religion and Spirituality in 2011 (Vieten et al., 2013). Interestingly, based on rigorous triangulation of a variety of mixed methods to examine the distinction between spirituality and religion, Streib and Hood (2016) find that it is not only unnecessary to establish spirituality as a separate or opposite concept, but also that it is not meaningful to study spirituality detached from religion. Instead, they argue, that there is a big overlap between religion and spirituality conceptually that could be better captured by the vertical (explicitly religious) and horizontal (implicitly religious) private experience of transcendence.

For many years, Division 36 also strongly advocated for the field of psychology to include religion under the rubric of cultural diversity in the APA's multicultural competency guidelines and training (e.g., American Psychological Association, 2002; American Psychological Association 2009). Based on his review, however, Belzen (2010) describes that there does not seem to be much of a relationship between cultural psychology and psychology of religion; hardly any cultural psychology theories have been applied to any religious phenomenon, and studies on religion conducted from a cultural psychology viewpoint are very limited. While collaboration on both sides would be desirable, he explains psychology of religion is a discipline more urgently in need of radical change: "as no single form of religious functioning is universal, and as no single form of religious psychic functioning can be properly understood without taking cultural factors into account," psychology of religion must move toward "cultural inclusiveness in its theories and methods" (p. 17).

Belzen (2001) points out that Wundt and other psychologists in the early modern period at the turn of the nineteenth century recognized religion as a cultural phenomenon and studied religiosity as a higher psychic process involving culture. Because religiosity is "a culturally constituted phenomenon in which psychic life expresses itself," Belzen (2010) explains that the object of psychology of religion is "a product of culture" (p. 25). In fact, he believes religion is one of the most complex aspects of human cultures. Recognizing people's definition of self, identity, conduct, and experience are all deeply intertwined with a given culture or particular "form of life" (Wittenstein, 1968), Belzen suggests individuals cannot be studied in isolation using laboratory experiments or questionnaires common to psychology of religion research. Study of individuals needs to utilize methods such as participant observation, interviews, and focus groups that allow religious beliefs, values, and acts rooted in a particular context or tradition to be investigated as a whole. He states there is no such thing as studying "religion" in general, but only an in depth analysis of some concrete phenomena belonging to a particular religious form of life. Because cultural psychology involves a detailed analysis of the unique effect of cultural context and its various manifestations in human psychic functioning, it requires a research approach that is flexible and sensitive to detect the impact of cultural-historical changes and the way they are socially organized and embodied at the psychological level (Pak, 2017).

In order to gain respectability, however, psychology of religion and spirituality adapted mainstream psychological methods based on the natural science tradition rather than embracing methods appropriate for topics unique to the field (Hood, 2013). The process of making psychology pursue abstract universal laws resulted in eliminating central human functions such as consciousness, intention, meaning, and religion. Because the natural science paradigm only permitted a narrow range of phenomena to be studied, researchers were denied the possibility of studying the rich mental phenomena people experience everyday (O'Neill, 2002). Lear (2014) interestingly takes William James' famous work to show a rare exception of how qualitative approaches were employed to explore overlooked phenomenon such as conscious experience, which led to the advancement of psychological science more than a century later; thus, he concludes, the most valuable contribution researchers can make for the discipline is not just being a technician but overcoming blindness by "seeing and giving names to things unknown" (p. 29) and putting forward new concepts and possibilities for the field to develop.

While numerous recommendations brought attention to the broader theoretical and methodological vision of the discipline that was present since the inception, the psychological study of religion and spirituality has always been dominated by quantitative approaches, largely employing questionnaires and scales (Belzen & Hood, 2006; Hood, 2013). In a 25-year review of leading publications in psychology of religion and spirituality (1978–2003), Aten and Hernandez (2005) discovered that only 22 out of the 2,726 articles used qualitative or mixed methods. Despite numerous calls for a multidisciplinary paradigm and pluralistic methodology by experts in psychology of religion (Emmons & Paloutzian 2003, Belzen & Hood, 2006; Belzen, 2010), analysis of the first four years of the *Psychology of Religion and Spirituality* (2008–2012), the official journal for the APA Division 36, shows that only eight of the 77 published studies were qualitative research (Leach & Soto, 2013).

Wulff (2003) describes the current state of psychology of religion research as one in "crisis" that needs to "start over" as the field has lost its theoretical depth and methodological breadth. Although the dominance of positivism and natural science restricted the advancement of integration of religion, the percentage of experimental studies continues to increase in major journals in spite of growing critiques (Belzen & Hood, 2006). Based on their review, Emmons and Paloutzian (2003) comment on the limited applicability of experimental methods and the old emphasis on measurement (e.g., Goursuch, 1984) that still dominated the field despite the call for methodological pluralism and interdisciplinary integration. Hood et al. (2018) similarly pointed out the ongoing problem of over reliance on scales in psychology of religion and spirituality research even though recommendations have been repeatedly made to recognize the limits of measures in general and diverse cultural and religious settings in particular.

Belzen and Hood (2006) note it is impossible for the discipline to advance knowledge by over-valuing laboratory studies as only empirical research and disdaining other approaches; instead these authors strongly advocate that in order to produce a real paradigm shift in the field, it is crucial to orient toward the hermeneutical or qualitative tradition and pay more attention to the particularities of religion and spirituality in the real-world context. More specifically, they argue, unlike the lower level structure (e.g., behaviorism, computational cognitive psychology), theories at the higher level increasingly require integration of human consciousness, culture, and history and a multilevel interdisciplinary paradigm in order to adequately capture and interpret the activities and experiences studied. Human lives must be situated and understood in specific cultural, historical, and religious settings. Thus, methodological pluralism has been emphasized to develop an integrative paradigm for the study of the psychology of religion and spirituality. Hood (2013) suggests if no single methodology or ontological position is privileged, then research questions will ideally guide selecting a method appropriate to answer and reveal truths without unnecessarily restricting the investigation. Given the current state of research, however, it is not surprising to learn that psychologists outside of the U.S. find America's massive production and obsession with quantitative data seldom applicable to their local contexts (Arnett, 2008; Gergen, Gulerce, Lock, & Misra, 1996). Methodological pluralism is imperative in order for psychology of religion and spirituality to survive and find relevance, especially in this era of rapid globalization.

3 Review of Qualitative Research in Psychology of Religion

Belzen (2010) has proposed that because religiosity is "a culturally constituted phenomenon in which psychic life expresses itself," the object of psychology of religion is a "product of culture" (p. 25). However, Pak (2017) has asserted that a problem within psychology of religion is that it has followed general trends of natural science focusing on experimental and quantitative measurement while neglecting the cultural character of an individual's development. As a solution, qualitative inquiry, designed to explore and understand specific religious forms of life that give meaning within a cultural context, has been proposed. Cultural psychology of religion has the potential to extract the nuanced meanings of religious and spiritual phenomena in the human psyche.

3.1 *Varieties of Qualitative Approaches*

There are various paradigms, or "set of interrelated assumptions about the social world which provides a philosophical and conceptual framework for the organized study of that world" (Filstead, 1979, p. 34), that can guide this investigation. Ponterotto (2005) has outlined four major paradigms: (1) positivism, (2) postpositivism, (3) constructivism-interpretivism, and (4) critical-ideological. The former two, guiding quantitative research, are distinct from the latter two, anchoring qualitative inquiry, in goals, ideographic (individual) and nomothetic (focused on discovering general patterns of behavior) orientations (Hood & Johnson, 1997), and etic (universal that applies to all humans) and emic (unique to individual, sociocultural) constructs (Pedersen, 1999). Positivism and postpositivism focus on predicting and controlling phenomena and emphasize cause-effect, generalization, and objective researcher role. They are both nomothetic and etic. Constructivism-interpretivism seeks to investigate the reality constructed in the mind of the individuals (Hansen, 2004) through deep reflection, extracted through dialogue between researcher and participant in co-constructed findings, and assumes that human perception is not only from the senses, but also from the brain as it processes the information into a reality (Kant 1881/1966). It is ideographic and emic, and it serves as the primary foundation for qualitative research methods. Critical-ideological strives to disrupt status quo (Kincheloe & McLaren, 1944, 2000) towards emancipation from oppression and transformation to a more egalitarian and democratic social order and understands that reality is constructed though power relations within social-historical context (Kemmis & McTaggart, 2000).

In addition, ideographic and emic serve as the conceptual base for multicultural qualitative research (e.g., feminist, critical race, queer theories). To facilitate rich cultural investigation, one cannot apply positivist research methods to qualitative inquiry because the former seeks to achieve predictability and generalizability while the latter aims to investigate deeper meaning and experience while capturing trends (Gergen, 2014; Pak, 2017). However, Ponterotto (2005) has expressed concern over a growing number of counseling psychologists who are unknowingly "'postpositivizing' constructivist qualitative methods" (p. 127), often in the form of literature driven, detailed, and standard semi-structured interviews; pre-selection of sample without theoretical sampling; pre-set theme categories before research; and calculation of the number of participants who are represented in each theme. In fact, he has asserted that many have adopted qualitative methods without understanding the philosophical anchors that impact the inquiry.

In-depth investigation into religion, spirituality, and culture necessitates the extraction of descriptions that integrate observations of human action within the cultural milieu that gives meaning to the actions, or "thick descriptions" (Lincoln & Guba, 1985; Geertz, 1973; Ryle, 1949). Introduced by philosopher Gilbert Ryle (1949), "thin descriptions" are surface-level observations of human behavior, and "thick descriptions" add context to those behaviors. Thus, Geertz (1973), in his adaptation of Ryle's original notion, argues that the study of culture is an interpretive process that is not only an observation of an action (e.g., the contraction of one eyelid), but also an interpretation of the action based on the cultural, social context (e.g., an eye twitch vs. a wink). Resisting reductionism, thick descriptions provide the information necessary to draw new knowledge (i.e., fresh insight, information, perspective) (Saldaña, 2011). This nuanced investigation has increased utility for the investigation of religion, which Belzen (2010) believes is "one of the most complex aspects of human cultures" (p. 174).

3.2 *Purpose of the Project: Exploring Truly Existing Qualitative Studies in Current Psychology of Religion*

With the potential that qualitative inquiry possesses to provide insight into culturally nuanced experiences, the present project explored the current status of qualitative research in psychology of religion and investigated how qualitative inquiry is utilized in the disciplinary area in recent decades. Qualitative studies on psychology and religion published in major journals in the last two decades were examined based on the following questions: (1) How frequently was qualitative research published in the journal? (2) What paradigm guided the qualitative investigation? What types of qualitative research methods were employed? (3) How many articles provided a research question and rationale for the qualitative research design selected? (4) How was the subject of religion and spirituality investigated in the cultural context?

3.3 *Method*

For this investigation, qualitative articles within six psychology of religion journals were selected and assessed based on (1) types of qualitative research paradigm, methods, and analysis (deductive vs. inductive); (2) quality and fit of the selected approach; and (3) adequacy of investigation covering psychology of religion/spirituality (R/S) and culture. The procedure is outlined below.

3.3.1 Journal Selection Criteria

To our knowledge, there has been only one previous review of qualitative research on religion and spirituality to date. Aten and Hernandez (2005) performed a 25-year review of qualitative studies published in spiritually and psychologically oriented peer-reviewed journals and found that "of the 2,726 titles published in the seven journals that were searched, only 22 (.008%) qualitative articles were located" (p. 266). Because qualitative research was remarkably underrepresented in these journals they identified as accounting for "a majority of the research published on spiritual and religious issues within the field of psychology" (p. 267), we included many of the previously reviewed journals for the present study to see what progress has been made in this area.

The American Psychological Association (APA) Division 36 is an important society, established in 1976 during the increasing trend of psychology of religion research (Emmons & Palouzian, 2003); for this reason, the divisional journal, *Psychology of Religion and Spirituality* (PORS), was also included in our analysis. Although the *Journal of Psychology & Theology* (JPT) and *Journal of Psychology and Christianity* (JPC) are limited to Christian faith, these two journals were selected because they were included in the previous review (Aten & Hernandez, 2005) and are recognized as long standing journals within psychology of religion (Paloutzian & Park, 2013). Similarly, *Pastoral Psychology* (PP), was also included in this review as it is one of the oldest journals in this topic area being founded in 1950. Additionally, though the journals *Mental Health, Religion & Culture* (MHRC) and *International Journal for Psychology of Religion* (IJPOR) both have a more international focus, they were selected not only because they were included in the previous review, but also because of their collaboration with PORS and APA Division 36. However, because the scope of this project was limited to the field of American psychology of religion, prominent international psychology of religion journals, such as *Archive for the Psychology of Religion*, were excluded from our present review.

Thus, the journals selected for the present review included: (1) *Psychology of Religion and Spirituality*, (2) *Journal of Psychology and Theology*, (3) *Journal of Psychology and Christianity*, (4) *Pastoral Psychology*, (5) *Mental Health, Religion & Culture*, and (6) *International Journal for the Psychology of Religion* (see Table 1 for summary information on these selected journals). All the qualitative research articles published in these six journals over the past 20 years were examined. After omitting theoretical and non-empirical articles, a total of 177 qualitative studies were reviewed.

3.3.2 Qualitative Article Review Evaluation Criteria

All the qualitative articles identified in each journal related to psychology and religion were reviewed and coded based on relevant categories identified for the purpose noted above. The primary author worked with the co-author in coding qualitative research articles over the course of a year. Engaged in multiple iterations of analysis, the authors collaborated in ongoing meetings to reach a consensus on the categories for coding and to discuss article quality for increased internal validity. Based on the research questions, the following criteria and coding categories were developed: (1) types of qualitative research paradigm, methods, and analysis (deductive vs. inductive); (2) quality and fit of the selected approach; and (3) adequacy of investigation covering psychology of religion/spirituality (R/S) and culture. The definition of each criteria, its foundation, and the coding procedures will be explained below.

3.3.2.1 *Paradigm*

While there are standards of trustworthiness that apply across all qualitative research, there are also particular standards congruent to specific paradigms; thus, not only do researchers have the task of basing their research question on theories behind the topic of inquiry, but they also should ground qualitative research within the paradigm that is most pertinent to the question and apply its standards for trustworthiness (Morrow, 2005; see also Ponterotto, 2005). Therefore, it is important to communicate in the article which paradigm is guiding the research. In light of this, the following two items related to paradigm were coded: (1) whether or not the paradigm was explicitly stated in the study; and (2) which of the three major paradigms in qualitative inquiry identified by Morrow (2005) and Ponterotto (2005) (i.e., postpositivism (PP), interpretivism-constructivism (IC), critical-ideological (CI)) was used.

If the article did not indicate a paradigm, one was assigned based on the research description provided. PP was assigned for studies that were hypothesis-driven, reductive in the data analysis portion (e.g., counting and comparing frequencies), and not in-depth in their analysis, results, or discussion. IC was assigned to articles that sought to gain insight into complex experiences with an inductive approach that emerged from the experiences of the participants. CI was assigned to articles that met all the criteria for IC and additionally sought social change. Multiple paradigms were noted for some mixed-methods studies (e.g., quantitative portion as positivist/postpositivist and the qualitative portion as constructivist).

3.3.2.2 *Big Q/Little Q: Inductive vs. Deductive*

Further, Kidder and Fine (1978) highlighted the two major research traditions in qualitative inquiry: (1) hypothetical, deductive methods, termed "little q," and (2) open-ended, inductive methods, termed "big Q." Articles were categorized as "little q" if they were conducting a deductive analysis, applying a priori themes and categories to the data (q) and as "big Q" if they were conducting an inductive analysis by allowing themes and meaning to emerge from the data (Q).

3.3.2.3 *Qualitative Research Methods*

There is a myriad of qualitative research methods designed to address diverse research questions. Within psychology of religion, Belzen and Hood (2006) have proposed that there are three types of research with different aims (i.e., relationship between psychic functioning and religiosity; how religion becomes part of a person's psychic make-up; and psychic components in religious phenomena) with no single method that can cut through them. To capture which methods were currently being employed in the field of psychology of religion, articles were coded deductively (based on prior knowledge of trends) and inductively (emerging), with codes created inductively applied back to all articles. They were coded as follows: consensual qualitative research (CQR; Hill et al., 2005; Hill, Thompson, & William, 1997), grounded theory (Glaser & Strauss, 1967; Charmaz, 2000, 2006), thematic analysis, content analysis, interpretive phenomenological analysis (IPA; Smith, 1996), phenomenological, hermeneutic, narrative, case study, ethnography, participatory action research (PAR), and mixed-methods. Articles that employed a method outside of these designated codes were placed in the "other" category. A number of articles that utilized the "constant comparative method" (Glaser & Strauss, 1967) were coded as grounded theory. Further, since researchers may have utilized more than one method in qualitative inquiry (e.g., one method to collect data and another for analysis), all methods in the articles were coded.

3.3.2.4 *Quality*

Further, measures of quality were assessed by examining the statement of research question(s), transparency, rationale, and fit. While quantitative research tests hypotheses, qualitative inquiry is designed to examine research questions. Distinct from the study aim, the research question outlines and defines the investigation and drives data collection and analysis. The articles were coded as having an explicit statement of the research question, hypothesis, or neither.

Morrow (2005) has suggested the following transcendent criteria for evaluating qualitative research regardless of the paradigm: social validity, subjectivity and reflexivity, adequacy of data, and adequacy of interpretation. These criteria can only be assessed through adequacy in transparency of the research process. In their groundbreaking call to the field of psychology of religion to utilize qualitative inquiry in pursuit of a deeper understanding of human religious/spiritual experience, Belzen and Hood (2006) assert that "transparency is regarded as more relevant than objectivity and is understood as bringing the research process into the open instead of chasing an unattainable ideal of neutralizing the interaction between researcher and research participant" (p. 19). Thus, transparency as a measure of accountability should include full detail of the research methods, including the data collection process, analysis, and results. Articles that provided detailed accounts of their research methodology were deemed to have high transparency. Articles with low transparency either: (1) did not specify their methodology, even when they specified a qualitative method but did not detail the process, or (2) offered very little details on their research methods.

A rationale for the use of qualitative inquiry in fulfilling research goals should be provided. Further, how the selected method is well-suited for the research question should be also explained in the rationale. Articles were deemed to present a rationale if they offered a reason for either employing a certain research method or qualitative inquiry for their topic of study.

3.3.2.5 *Fit*

In qualitative inquiry, there should be a coherence between the research question and design. As Flyvbjerg (2006) proposes, "good social science is problem driven and not methodology driven in the sense that it employs methods that for a given problem, best help answer the research question at hand" (p. 242). Articles that did so were deemed to have high fit. For instance, if the research question calls for an exploration into the meaning of an experience, a method that is able to draw out the nuance of the meaning (e.g., phenomenological or narrative) would be considered a good fit. Articles that did not show coherence were considered to be low fit (e.g., an in-depth research question answered through deductive content analysis). If the research question, the purpose, and/or the research design were unstated, the fit was undeterminable.

3.3.2.6 *Religion/Spirituality and Culture: Degrees of Depth of Analysis*

The preceding qualitative inquiry standards of quality ultimately informed assessment of the adequacy of the examination of religious and spiritual issues and culture. Articles were categorized into three groups: (1) good, in-depth analysis (based on above categories), (2) some in-depth analysis, and (3) no in-depth analysis. Specifically, articles that selected a qualitative method that allowed for themes to emerge through inductive study and explored the nuance and meaning of experience as embedded in a cultural context were deemed to produce thick descriptions (Geertz, 1973; Ryle, 1949) and considered in-depth in study. Articles that only produced thin descriptions (e.g., conducted from a deductive, postpositivist standpoint; sought to confirm a hypothesis; did not present a robust discussion from the findings) were considered to not have in-depth analysis.

3.4 *Results*

In this section, findings from each journal are presented. Journal information and the percentage of qualitative articles within the journal are given, followed by an examination of qualitative paradigms and methodology, quality and fit, and the treatment of culture and religion/spirituality. It concludes with a summary of all six journals (see Table 2).

3.4.1 Psychology of Religion and Spirituality (PORS)

First, *Psychology of Religion and Spirituality* (PORS) was examined. PORS is a quarterly, peer-reviewed journal of psychology of religion and spirituality published by APA Division 36, The Society for the Psychology of Religion and Spirituality. Publication began in 2009 when it replaced the previous journal (*Psychology of Religion*) published by the division and continues to present. Qualitative articles in this journal focused on exploring the religious and spiritual experiences of all religious traditions. Out of 363 total articles published between 2008–2019, only 32 were qualitative. Though the proportion of qualitative articles were still less than a tenth (8.82%) of the entire journal, it had the greatest proportion of qualitative studies among the six journals.

3.4.1.1 *Paradigm*

QR studies from this journal were overwhelmingly conducted from a postpositivist paradigm (N = 25; 78.13%). Eight of them were conducted from an interpretive-constructivist paradigm (25.00%), with only one of these explicitly stating the paradigm in the entire journal (3.13%), revealing the positivist leaning in the journal. There were no critical ideological articles.

3.4.1.2 *Big Q/Little Q Research Tradition*

More studies were conducted deductively (N = 12; 37.50%) than inductively (N = 9; 28.13%). Some did both (N = 9; 28.13%).

3.4.1.3 *Qualitative Research Methods*

Three quarters of the articles clearly stated their research method (*N* = 24; 75.00%). Of the qualitative methods, grounded theory (*N* = 11; 34.38) was the most popular, closely followed by thematic analysis (*N* = 10; 31.25%) and content analysis (*N* = 8; 25.00%). However, many of the studies claiming to utilize grounded theory methods appeared to utilize thematic analysis, evidenced by a lack of consolidated theory or model generated from the themes. Only a handful of articles utilized methods that normally seek more in-depth analysis: phenomenological (*N* = 3; 9.38%), narrative (*N* = 4; 12.50%), ethnography (*N* = 2; 6.25%), hermeneutic (*N* = 1; 3.13%), PAR (*N* = 1; 3.13%), and case study (*N* = 1; 3.13). CQR was used once (3.13%), and there was one article that fell into the other category (3.13%). Further, over half of the articles were a type of mixed-methods (*N* = 18; 56.25%). However, more than half of the mixed-methods (*N* = 11) were merely an analysis of an open-ended question at the end of a survey. Some of the other mixed-method articles used semi-structured interviews with their participants to collect data, with some that pursued in-depth analysis and others that did not.

3.4.1.4 *Quality*

A little less than half of the studies (*N* = 15, 46.88%) stated their research question, four proposed hypotheses (12.50%), and 13 stated neither (40.63%). About four out of ten articles showed good transparency (*N* = 14; 43.75%), but a quarter of the articles showed no transparency at all (*N* = 8; 25.00%). One out of seven articles showed some transparency (*N* = 5; 15.63%). Less than a quarter of the articles (*N* = 7; 21.88) gave a rationale for their use of qualitative inquiry and/or of their qualitative methods.

3.4.1.5 *Fit*

With the high frequency of postpositivist methodology, there was a low percentage of articles that demonstrated good fit between research question and methods chosen (*N* = 6; 18.75%). More than half of the studies did not demonstrate a good fit (*N* = 20; 62.50%). Due to the lack of transparency or research question, the fit for six articles could not be determined (*N* = 6; 18.75%).

3.4.1.6 *Religion/Spirituality and Culture: Degrees of Depth of Analysis*

Though a large percentage touched on some religious experience and attempted to gain some insight (*N* = 25, 78.13%), surprisingly, only five articles (15.63%) truly conducted an in-depth study of religious and spiritual issues. Further, only three articles (9.38%) considered culture in any depth, while six did some (18.75%); an overwhelming 23 articles (71.88%) did not address cultural context at all in investigating religion and spirituality.

3.4.2 International Journal for Psychology of Religion (IJPOR)

In order to compare the quality of qualitative inquiry in psychology of religion, an international journal was also included. IJPOR is a quarterly, peer-reviewed international journal that focuses on psychological studies of religious processes and phenomena in all religious traditions. It is affiliated with APA Division 36 and the International Association for the Psychology of Religion (IAPR). From 2001–2018, it published 355 total articles. Only seven of these articles (1.97%) were qualitative studies.

3.4.2.1 *Paradigm*

More studies were conducted from an interpretive-constructivist paradigm ($N = 4$; 57.15%) than postpositivism (PP; $N = 3$; 42.86%) but differed only by one. There were no articles from a critical-ideological paradigm. Only one article explicitly stated its paradigm.

3.4.2.2 *Big Q/Little Q Research Tradition*

All four of the interpretive-constructivist articles used an inductive approach for data collection and analysis. Two of the postpositivist articles used a deductive approach ($N = 2$; 28.57%), and one utilized both (14.29%). One of these articles explicitly stated its use of a constructivist paradigm.

3.4.2.3 *Qualitative Research Methods*

On the other hand, only one article did not state its method. Phenomenological ($N = 3$; 42.86%) was the most popular, followed by narrative ($N = 2$; 28.57%), IPA ($N = 1$; 14.29%), hermeneutic ($N = 1$; 14.29%), and ethnography ($N = 1$; 14.29%). Two of the studies were mixed-methods ($N = 2$; 28.57%).

3.4.2.4 *Quality*

Less than half these articles stated a research question ($N = 3$; 42.86%). One stated a hypothesis (14.29%), and three stated neither (42.86%). All seven of the articles demonstrated good transparency (100.00%). A little less than half of the articles offered a rationale for their use of qualitative methods ($N = 3$; 42.86%).

3.4.2.5 *Fit*

A majority of the articles demonstrated good fit ($N = 4$; 57.14%), and only one of them showed low fit. However, due to a lack of transparency, the fit for two articles could not be determined ($N = 2$; 28.57%).

3.4.2.6 *Religion/Spirituality and Culture: Degrees of Depth of Analysis*

This journal produced the highest percentage of in-depth articles on religion and spirituality (*N* = 5; 71.43%). The rest of the articles showed some (*N* = 2; 28.57%). On the other hand, only one article studied culture in-depth (14.29%), and the others did some (14.29%). The rest (*N* = 5; 71.43%) did not address culture.

3.4.3 Journal of Psychology and Theology (JPT)

The *Journal of Psychology and Theology* (JPT) is a quarterly, peer-reviewed journal that focuses on publishing research on the integration of psychology and Christian theology. Both empirical and theoretical articles are considered for publication, though the former is preferred. The interrelationships of psychology and theology that are explored are applied to various contexts (e.g., mental health, counseling, education and training, ministry). This journal produced articles that were specific to experiences in religious contexts (e.g., church, academia, counseling, mission field). JPT published 1043 articles between 1999 and 2017, of which only 34 (3.26%) were qualitative articles.

3.4.3.1 *Paradigm*

Only two articles (5.88%) within the journal stated their paradigm, both of which were interpretive-constructivist. The rest were assigned based on research description, of which more than half (*N* = 22; 64.71%) of the articles were conducted within a postpositivist framework, while around a third (*N* = 12; 35.29%) were from an interpretive-constructivist paradigm. There were none from a critical-ideological paradigm.

3.4.3.2 *Big Q/Little Q Research Tradition*

More studies were conducted from the Big Q research tradition (*N* = 15; 44.12%) than the little q research tradition (*N* = 12; 35. 29%). About an eighth (*N* = 6; 17.65%) utilized both.

3.4.3.3 *Qualitative Research Methods*

Most of the articles stated their method explicitly (*N* = 31; 91.18%). The most popular was grounded theory (*N* = 7; 20.59%), phenomenological (*N* = 7; 20.59%), and mixed methods (*N* = 7; 20.59%), with about a fifth utilizing each, followed by content analysis (*N* = 6; 17.65%), thematic analysis (*N* = 4; 11.76%), narrative (*N* = 3; 8.82%), ethnography (*N* = 3; 8.82%), CQR (*N* = 3; 8.82%), case study (*N* = 2; 5.88%), hermeneutic (*N* = 2; 5.88%), and other (*N* = 3; 8.82%). PAR was utilized once (2.94%). A little less than half of the articles that utilized mixed-methods (*N* = 3; 42.86%) merely analyzed open-ended survey questions rather than seeking in-depth data collection. The methods for five articles (14.71%) were undeterminable due to lack of transparency.

3.4.3.4 *Quality*

Strikingly, almost three-quarters ($N = 25$; 73.53%) of the articles failed to state a research question. About a fifth of the overall articles ($N = 9$; 17.65%) stated a hypothesis instead of a research question, and a majority stated neither ($N = 19$; 55.88), leaving only about a quarter that stated the research question explicitly ($N = 9$; 26.47%). About a third of the articles demonstrated good transparency with their methods and overall research process ($N = 11$; 32.35%). About a quarter showed some level of transparency ($N = 9$; 26.47%), and a fifth showed no transparency at all with regards to the research process ($N = 7$; 20.59%). A third of the articles also provided a clear rationale for the use of qualitative inquiry for their topic of research and/or for the specific method ($N = 11$; 32.35%).

3.4.3.5 *Fit*

Less than a third of the articles demonstrated a coherent fit ($N = 10$; 29.41%), while over half of them did not ($N = 18$; 52.94%). The fit was indeterminable for six articles (17.65%) due to the lack of transparency or an explicit research question.

3.4.3.6 *Religion/Spirituality and Culture: Degrees of Depth of Analysis*

A little less than a third successfully conducted an in-depth study of religion ($N = 10$; 29.41%). About half of the articles ($N = 19$; 55.88%) studied religion to some degree, and some did not address it at all in an in-depth way ($N = 5$; 14.71). Furthermore, an overwhelming majority did not demonstrate adequacy in the investigation of culture, with almost three-fourths failing to even acknowledge the impact of culture on the study ($N = 24$; 70.59%). Only a small percentage briefly acknowledged it ($N = 4$; 11.76%). Less than a fifth produced in-depth fresh insight into cultural experience ($N = 6$; 17.65%).

3.4.4 Journal of Psychology and Christianity (JPC)

Journal of Psychology and Christianity (JPC) is a quarterly, peer-reviewed journal published by the Christian Association of Psychological Studies (CAPS). Publication began in 1982 and continues to present. It focuses on topics of interest to Christian professionals in psychological and pastoral professions by addressing: (1) issues in psychology that can be useful to Christian academic and applied settings, (2) the relationship between psychology and Christian faith, (3) clinical practice, and (4) application of psychology to the work of Christian organizations. The qualitative articles within the journal focused on a mixture of Christian religious/spiritual experiences (e.g., conversion, forgiveness, prayer) and experiences specific to religious organization (e.g., corporate worship, clergy). Within the journal from 2006 to 2018, there were 30 qualitative empirical studies among 567 published articles (5.29%).

3.4.4.1 *Paradigm*

There was about an even split between postpositivist ($N = 15$; 50.00%) and interpretive-constructivist ($N = 16$; 53.33%) studies. There were no articles from a critical-ideological paradigm. Only one of the constructivist articles explicitly stated its paradigm (3.33%).

3.4.4.2 *Big Q/Little Q Research Tradition*

Two-thirds of articles conducted inductive studies ($N = 20$; 66.67%), while one-third ($N = 10$; 33.33%) conducted deductive studies.

3.4.4.3 *Qualitative Research Methods*

Most of the articles explicitly stated a method ($N = 27$; 90.00%). The most popular was grounded theory, with almost half of the articles utilizing this approach ($N = 13$; 43.44%). It was followed by content analysis ($N = 6$; 20.00%), phenomenological ($N = 6$; 20.00%), and mixed-methods ($N = 5$; 16.67%). Two of these "mixed-methods" were merely an analysis of open-ended survey questions. The other methods were not as popular: thematic analysis ($N = 3$; 10.00%), IPA ($N = 2$; 6.67%), and case study ($N = 1$; 3.33%). Three studies used other methods (10.00%). The methods used in two of the articles could not be determined (6.67%).

3.4.4.4 *Quality*

Half of the articles stated a research question ($N = 15$; 50.00%), one stated a hypothesis (3.33%), and a little less than half did not state either ($N = 14$; 46.67%). More than half of the articles showed good transparency ($N = 17$; 56.67%), while only one had none (3.33%). A third ($N = 11$; 36.67%) had some transparency. A little over a third of the articles provided a rationale ($N = 11$; 36.67%).

3.4.4.5 *Fit*

The fit was indeterminable for about a fifth of the articles ($N = 7$; 23.33%). However, among the articles that could be determined for fit, there was about an even split between those that demonstrated good fit ($N = 12$; 40.00%) and low fit ($N = 11$; 36.36%).

3.4.4.6 *Religion/Spirituality and Culture: Degrees of Depth of Analysis*

Similar to other journals, though the majority addressed religion to some degree ($N = 18$; 60.00%), only one in every five articles studied religion in-depth ($N = 6$; 20.00%). Six articles did not address religion at all (20.00%) by focusing only on the psychological phenomena (e.g., conflict, coping) within an institutional context and not addressing the psychic religious, spiritual dimensions of experience. Further, only three articles adequately investigated the cultural context (10.00%), and one did some (3.33%). A large majority did not address culture ($N = 26$; 86.67%).

3.4.5 Pastoral Psychology

Started in 1950, *Pastoral Psychology* (PP) is one of the oldest psychology of religion/spirituality journals. It is a quarterly, peer-reviewed journal that integrates psychological, behavioral, social, and human sciences with issues of pastoral care and ministry (e.g., pastors' kids, clergy relocation, church members). It publishes articles on all psychological, theoretical, and religious/spiritual perspectives. Within this journal, between 1998 and 2018, there were only 28 qualitative studies among the 5670 total published articles (0.49%), possessing the lowest proportion of qualitative studies among the journals.

3.4.5.1 *Paradigm*

Eleven articles were conducted from an interpretive-constructivist paradigm (39.29%). Only two of these articles stated a paradigm (7.14%). About two-thirds of the articles ($N = 19$; 67.86%) were conducted from a postpositivist paradigm. There were none from the critical-ideological paradigm.

3.4.5.2 *Big Q/Little Q Research Tradition*

More articles conducted an inductive analysis ($N = 16$, 57.14%) in comparison to deductive analysis ($N = 11$, 39.29%). One used both.

3.4.5.3 *Qualitative Research Methods*

Grounded theory was the most popular with about a third of the studies ($N = 9$; 32.14%) utilizing this approach followed by mixed methods ($N = 5$; 17.86%). Two of these mixed methods were merely an analysis of open-ended survey questions. The remaining articles used the following: thematic analysis ($N = 3$; 10.71%), narrative ($N = 3$; 10.71%), IPA ($N = 3$; 10.71%), phenomenological ($N = 2$; 7.14%), ethnography ($N = 2$; 7.14%), and content analysis ($N = 2$; 7.14%). Two studies used other methods (7.14%). The methods of six articles could not be determined (17.86%).

3.4.5.4 *Quality*

Only nine of these articles stated a research question (32.14%), two stated a hypothesis (7.14%), and 17 stated neither (60.71%). A little over a third ($N = 10$; 35.71%) demonstrated good transparency with their methods, while another third ($N = 10$; 35.71%) showed none. The rest landed somewhere in between ($N = 8$; 28.57%). Further, less than a fifth of the studies gave a clear rationale for their use of qualitative inquiry and the specific qualitative method selected ($N = 5$; 17.86%).

3.4.5.5 *Fit*

A little over a quarter of the studies showed a good fit between their research question and/or aim ($N = 8$; 28.57%), while exactly a quarter of studies did not demonstrate a good fit between their research question and methods ($N = 7$; 25.00%). The fit was indeterminable for twelve of the articles (42.86%) because of a lack of research question or lack of transparency in their methodology.

3.4.5.6 *Religion/Spirituality and Culture: Degrees of Depth of Analysis*

Finally, only four of the articles (14.29%) conducted an in-depth analysis of religion and spirituality, though a number of them sought to do so to some extent ($N = 17$; 60.71%). Eight of the articles did not adequately address R/S ($N = 8$; 28.57%). Further, only two articles (7.14%) conducted an in-depth analysis of culture, and one did some (3.56%) revealing the many missed opportunities to delve deeper into these experiences. Almost nine out of 10 articles did not mention culture ($N = 25$; 89.29%).

3.4.6 Mental Health, Religion and Culture (MHRC)

Mental Health, Religion and Culture (MHRC) is an interdisciplinary, international peer-reviewed journal that publishes work that explores the relationship between mental health and various aspects of religion and culture. Issues are published 10 times a year, and publication began in 1998. The journal seeks to capture the intersection of mental health and religion by focusing on issues related to religious influences on mental health (e.g., psychiatric symptoms, coping, mental disorders, therapy), mental health as it influences thoughts about religion/spirituality, and the role of religious personnel in a mental health team. Between 1998 and 2017, out of 981 published articles in MHRC, there were 46 qualitative research articles (7.65%).

3.4.6.1 *Paradigm*

Though it was only one in seven articles within the journal, *MHRC* had the highest number of articles directly stating a paradigm out of all the journals ($N = 8$;

17.39%). In this journal, more people conducted a study from an interpretive-constructivist view (*N* = 30; 65.22%) than postpositivist (*N* = 20; 43.48%). None were critical-ideological.

3.4.6.2 *Big Q/Little Q Research Tradition*

Further, with almost three-fourths of the studies utilizing inductive methods to allow themes and theories to emerge from the data itself (*N* = 34; 73.91%), *MHRC* had the highest percentage of inductive methods among the journals. Only about a fifth of the articles used deductive methods exclusively (21.74%). Two articles used both (4.35%).

3.4.6.3 *Qualitative Research Methods*

Due to the lack of transparency and lack of stating the research question, the methods for eight of the articles could not be determined (17.39%). From the articles that stated a method and the ones in which method was determinable, there was a wider distribution between different methods. Thematic analysis (*N* = 8; 17.39%) was the most popular closely followed by grounded theory (*N* = 7; 15.22%), CQR (*N* = 6; 13.04%), phenomenological (*N* = 6; 13.04%), IPA (*N* = 6; 13.04%), narrative (*N* = 5; 10.87), case study (*N* = 4; 8.70%), mixed-methods (*N* = 4; 8.70%), ethnography (*N* = 1; 2.17%), hermeneutic (*N* = 1; 2.17%), and other (*N* = 6; 13.04%).

3.4.6.4 *Quality*

Out of the 46 articles, 16 stated an explicit research question (34.78%), two stated a hypothesis, and a large majority of 28 (60.87%) did not state either. This journal had the largest proportion of studies demonstrate good transparency (*N* = 19; 41.20%), with another large percentage (*N* = 15; 32.61%) showing some. However, seven of the articles did not show any transparency (*N* = 7; 15.22%). About a quarter of the articles provided a rationale for their usage of qualitative methods.

3.4.6.5 *Fit*

There were more articles that had a high fit (*N* = 20; 43.48%) than a low fit (*N* = 12; 26.09%), but it was still less than half. Further, the fit could not be determined for almost a third of the articles, mostly because the research questions were not stated.

3.4.6.6 *Religion/Spirituality and Culture: Degrees of Depth of Analysis*

In relation to the study of religion and spirituality, for every ten articles, four were conducted in-depth (*N* = 17; 36.96%), five touched on some in-depth themes ($N = 24$; 52.17%), and one did not go in-depth at all ($N = 5$; 10.86%). Further, among all the journals, *MHRC* had the most percentage of studies that examined culture in-depth ($N = 13$; 28.26%). However, still a majority did not address culture at all ($N = 29$; 63.04%), while a small minority mentioned it to some extent ($N = 4$; 8.70%).

3.4.7 Overall Summary of Findings

Altogether, the findings highlight the miniscule presence of qualitative articles published within the last two decades in major psychology of religion journals. Out of the 8,979 articles in the six journals, 177 were qualitative studies, accounting for only 1.97%. An overall landscape of the field is presented below.

3.4.7.1 *Paradigm*

Only fifteen articles explicitly stated a paradigm (8.47%), all of which were conducted from an interpretive-constructivist paradigm. Therefore, for a majority of the studies, the paradigms had to be identified based on the articles' statements of the research question, design, and methods. An analysis of the articles based on these factors revealed that more research was conducted from a postpositivist paradigm ($N = 104$; 58.76%) than an interpretive-constructionist paradigm ($N = 79$; 44.63%). There were none conducted from a critical-ideological paradigm.

3.4.7.2 *Big Q/Little q Research Tradition*

A little over half (55.93%) of the articles conducted an inductive study that allowed themes and analysis to emerge from the collected data, but about a third were doing deductive methods (32.20%). A tenth combined both methods (10.17%), most of which started inductively to create a list of themes for a codebook and then deductively coded all the data again from the created codes. Others conducted a mixed-method study with a combination of a quantitative, deductive design and a qualitative, inductive design. Though the majority of studies chose inductive methods to let themes emerge from the data, a majority of selected analyses only produced thin descriptions of the experience or phenomena under study.

3.4.7.3 *Qualitative Research Methods*

Overall, about four out of five articles explicitly stated their qualitative research method ($N = 145$; 81.92%). Though some of the remaining articles ($N = 32$; 18.08%) could be categorized, a majority of them could not be determined ($N = 22$; 12.43%), often due to a lack of transparency in their details of their research design and methodology. These articles often called their study "qualitative" but failed to state the method. Grounded theory was the most popular (*N* = 48; 27.12%), followed by mixed-methods (*N* = 41; 23.16%), thematic analysis (*N* = 29; 16.38%), phenomenological (*N* = 27; 15.25%), content analysis (*N* = 23; 12.99%), narrative (*N* = 19; 10.73), and other (*N* = 16; 9.04%). A small percentage utilized CQR (*N* = 11; 6.21%). The following methods were not highly utilized: IPA (*N* = 12; 6.78%), ethnography (*N* = 8; 4.52%), case study (*N* = 8; 4.52%), hermeneutic (*N* = 2; 1.13%), and PAR (*N* = 2; 1.13). The most popular interpretive-constructivist method was phenomenological (*N* = 27; 15.25%).

3.4.7.4 *Quality*

Strikingly, only 68 articles (38.42%) stated a clear research question, which is the equivalent of not stating a research hypothesis in quantitative studies. Some (*N* = 16; 9.04%) even stated a hypothesis for a qualitative inquiry. More than half did not state either (*N* = 94; 53.11%). Overall, the articles showed moderate transparency. Among the articles there were extreme differences. Seventy-eight articles offered good transparency (44.07%), offering meticulous detailing of their methods. On the other hand, 33 articles showed little to no transparency (18.64%). As a whole, it seemed that transparency increased over time, but even some more recent articles lacked transparency, especially if qualitative was embedded in a mixed-methods study. Around a quarter of the articles landed in the middle (*N* = 44, 24.86%). Only a little over a quarter of the articles (*N* = 49; 27.68%) provided a clear rationale for qualitative inquiry and the specific qualitative research design chosen.

3.4.7.5 *Fit*

Finally, in the present evaluation of the selection and implementation of research methods and design based on the research question, only about a third of all articles had a good fit (*N* = 60; 33.90%). A slightly larger number did not demonstrate coherence in research methods (*N* = 69; 38.98%). For a little over a quarter of the articles, the fit was indeterminable (*N* = 48; 27.12%) either because of a lack of transparency in their methods, a lack of an explicit statement of the research question, or both.

3.4.7.6 *Religion/Spirituality and Culture: Degrees of Depth of Analysis*

Finally, it was surprising to find that few articles sought to study the R/S experience in-depth within psychology and religion journals. Only about a quarter of the articles (*N* = 47; 26.55%) sought to gain fresh insight and deep understanding of religious/spiritual phenomena. More than half of the articles (*N* = 104; 58.76%) only provided moderate attempts to produce in-depth exploration of religion/spirituality. Finally, 26 of the articles (14.69%) did not engage with religion in an in-depth way but rather chose deductive methods that were mostly seeking to confirm a hypothesis or make generalizations. Even though culture and religion are deeply intertwined, and qualitative inquiry seeks to gain in-depth understanding of experience that exists at that intersection, only 28 articles (15.82%) engaged with culture in a meaningful way. Another 17 articles (9.60%) mentioned some, and the overwhelming majority (N = 132; 74.58%) did not interact with culture at all.

3.5 *Discussion*

3.5.1 Summary of Findings

In this section, a summary of the findings will be applied to answer the research questions and capture trends of qualitative inquiry in psychology of religion, concluding with a highlight of a few examples for future studies to follow. Table 1 provides a summary of the six selected journals.

TABLE 1 Summary information on six selected journals

Category	Journals					
	PORS	IJPOR	JPT	JPC	PP	MHRC
Publisher/ association	APA Division 36	Taylor & Francis	SAGE, Biola University	Christian Association for Psychological Studies	Springer	Routledge, Taylor & Francis
Country/ scope	USA	USA, international	USA	USA	USA, international	UK, international
Societies	APA Division 36	IAPR	None	Christian Association for Psychological Studies	None	APA Division 36; BACIP; IAPR; British Sociological Association; Spirituality & Psychiatry
Peer reviewed	Yes	Yes	Yes	Yes	Yes	Yes

TABLE 1 Summary information on six selected journals (*cont.*)

Category	Journals					
	PORS	IJPOR	JPT	JPC	PP	MHRC
History	2009–present	1991–present	1973–present	1982–present	1950–present	1998–present
Publishing frequency	Quarterly	Quarterly	Quarterly	Quarterly	Quarterly	10 Issues/year
H5-index factor	28	17	13	10	13	16
Multiple year impact factor	2.533 (5-year)	1.427 (5-year)	0.935 (5-year)	Not provided	0.530 (3-year)	0.670 (3-year)
Religious and spiritual traditions	All	All	Christianity	Christianity	All	All
Disciplines	Psychology, religion	Psychology, religion	Psychology, Christian theology, integration	Psychology, Christianity, integration	Psychology, religion, pastoral care	Interdisciplinary
Indexed in PsychInfo	Yes	Yes	Yes	Yes	Yes	Yes

Note: BACIP = British Association of Christians in Psychology; IAPR = International Association for the Psychology of Religion.

In response to the first research question, qualitative research made up a strikingly low 1.97% ($N = 177$) of the total 8,979 articles across the six journals in the last two decades. This highlighted the underutilization of qualitative methods in published psychology of religion articles thus far in the field.

The second question, related to the paradigm and type of qualitative methods utilized, was more challenging to answer. First, only 15 articles (8.47%) explicitly stated their paradigm; for a majority of the studies, paradigms needed to be deduced through the presented research design in the article. Further, more articles utilized a postpositivist (58.19%) than interpretive-constructivist paradigm (45.20%), with *POR/S* as high as 78.13% postpositivist and *IJPOR* low as 42.86% postpositivist. On the other hand, more articles conducted an inductive analysis (55.37%) than deductive analysis (32.20%). Some utilized both (10.73%). Though one may expect that an inductive analysis indicates an in-depth study that allows meanings and interpretations to emerge from the data (thus correlated with the interpretive-constructivist paradigm), this was not always the case. Many articles chose reductive methods in their data analysis using software programs such as *NVivo* and *ATLAS.ti* in their analysis. Though some studies used these programs as a way to organize meaning statements that they drew from in-depth interviews, a large number of the studies used them to merely code the frequency of words or phrases and to compare statistics. Though this technique could aid in certain types of qualitative methods, it does not yield thick descriptions of experiences.

The methods employed revealed the study aims and more postpositivist assumptions. Grounded theory (27.12%) and mixed methods (23.16%) were the most popular. Though there are two major forms of grounded theory—postpositivist and interpretive—the former was more popular among researchers. These observations were consistent with the findings that both thematic analysis (16.38%) and content analysis (12.99%) were the next most popular, all following the postpositivist tradition.

Additionally, the popularity of mixed methods may be due to the false belief that it is the "most robust" research method. On the contrary, Creswell and Plano Clark (2010) have cautioned that mixed methods should be employed with competent experience in both quantitative and qualitative methods and applied to the right research question (Pak, 2017). When done well, it can aid cultural researchers as one method offsets the weaknesses of the other. This means that a mixed method should contain both a quantitative and qualitative study, following standards for each with integrity. However, the mixed methods in this review came short of this standard. Almost half of the mixed-methods (and thus almost a tenth of all the qualitative articles) merely conducted an analysis of an open-ended question at the end of a quantitative survey for their qualitative portion. This data collection method does not lead to in-depth qualitative inquiry, for there are no opportunities for participants' meanings to emerge through a short answer. Furthermore, sometimes the quantitative sections did not meet their own standards of excellence. For example, some studies conducted a survey with a small sample size (i.e., less than 30) as their quantitative portion of their mixed-methods study, which does not produce strong validity.

Table 2 provides a summary of qualitative paradigms, methods, and quality in psychology of religion journals.

TABLE 2 Summary of qualitative research paradigm, method, and quality in psychology of religion journals

Category		Overall		Journal											
				POR/S (2008–2019)		IJPOR (2001–2018)		JPT (1999–2017)		JPC (2006–2018)		PP (1998–2019)		MHRC (1998–2017)	
		Count	% JN*	Count	% JN	Count	% JN	Count	% JN	Count	% JN	Count	% JN	Count	% JN
Descriptive	Total articles in journal	8,979		363		355		1043		567		5670		981	
	QR articles in journal	177	1.97	32	8.82	7	1.97	34	3.26	30	5.29	28	.49	46	25.99
		Count	% QR*	Count	% QR	Count	% QR	Count	% QR	Count	% QR	Count	% QR	Count	% QR
Paradigm	Postpositivism	104	58.76	25	78.13	3	42.86	22	64.71	15	50.00	18	64.29	21	45.65
	Interpretivism-constructivism	79	44.63	7	21.88	4	57.14	12	35.29	16	50.00	11	39.29	30	65.22
	Critical-ideological	0	0.00	0	0.00	0	0.00	0	0.00	0	0.00	0	0.00	0	0.00
q/Q	Deductive analysis	57	32.20	12	37.50	2	28.57	12	35.29	10	33.33	11	39.29	10	21.74
	Inductive analysis	98	55.37	9	28.13	4	57.14	15	44.12	20	66.67	16	57.14	34	73.91
	Both	19	10.73	9	28.13	1	14.29	6	17.65	0	0.00	1	3.57	2	4.35
Method	CQR	11	6.21	1	3.13	0	0.00	3	8.82	0	0.00	1	3.57	6	13.04
	Grounded theory	48	27.12	11	34.38	1	14.29	7	20.59	13	43.33	9	32.14	7	15.22
	Thematic analysis	29	16.38	10	31.25	1	14.29	4	11.76	3	10.00	3	10.71	8	17.39
	Content analysis	23	12.99	8	25.00	0	0.00	6	17.65	6	20.00	2	7.14	1	2.17

TABLE 2 Summary of qualitative research paradigm, method, and quality in psychology of religion journals (*cont.*)

Category		Overall		Journal											
				POR/S (2008–2019)		IJPOR (2001–2018)		JPT (1999–2017)		JPC (2006–2018)		PP (1998–2019)		MHRC (1998–2017)	
		Count	% JN*	Count	% JN	Count	% JN	Count	% JN	Count	% JN	Count	% JN	Count	% JN
	IPA	12	6.78	0	0.00	1	14.29	0	0.00	2	6.67	3	10.71	6	13.04
	Phenomenological	27	15.25	3	9.38	3	42.86	7	20.59	6	20.00	2	7.14	6	13.04
	Hermeneutic	5	2.83	1	3.13	1	14.29	2	5.88	0	0.00	0	0.00	1	2.17
	Narrative	19	10.73	4	12.50	2	28.57	3	8.82	2	6.67	3	10.71	5	10.87
	Case study	8	4.52	1	3.13	0	0.00	2	5.88	1	3.33	0	0.00	4	8.70
	Ethnographic	8	4.52	2	6.25	0	0.00	3	8.82	0	0.00	2	7.14	1	2.17
	PAR	2	1.13	1	3.13	0	0.00	1	2.94	0	0.00	0	0.00	0	0.00
	Mixed methods	41	23.16	18	56.25	2	28.57	7	20.59	5	16.67	5	17.86	4	8.70
	Other	16	9.04	10	31.25	1	14.29	3	8.82	3	10.00	2	7.14	6	13.04
Quality	Rationale	49	27.68	7	21.88	3	42.86	11	32.35	11	36.67	5	17.86	12	26.09
	Transparency	78	44.07	14	43.75	7	100.00	11	32.35	17	56.67	10	35.71	19	41.30
Fit	High	60	33.90	6	18.75	4	57.14	10	29.41	12	40.00	8	28.57	20	43.48
	Low	69	38.98	20	62.50	1	14.29	18	52.94	11	36.67	7	25.00	12	26.09
	Indeterminable**	48	27.12	6	18.75	2	28.57	6	17.65	7	23.33	13	46.43	14	30.43

Note: JN = journal; QR = qualitative research articles.
*% JN = the percentage of articles in each journal; % QR = the percentage of QR articles in each journal.
**Fit was undeterminable for articles without a research question or transparency.

Nonetheless, 45.20% of articles utilized an interpretive paradigm, seeking to understand the religious/spiritual experience, true to qualitative inquiry's emphasis on interpretation and understanding human action (Belzen, 2001; Browning, 2001; Denzin & Lincoln, 2000; Pak, 2017; Straub, 2006). Though still the minority, these studies sought to gain insight into religious/spiritual phenomena utilizing methods that allow for nuanced interpretation, such as phenomenological (12.25%), narrative (10.73%), IPA (6.78%), case study (4.52), ethnography (4.52%), hermeneutic, and PAR (1.13%). Given that a number of articles in the present review sought in-depth exploration into religious phenomena, these methods may have provided a better fit for the various research questions proposed throughout the articles. Increased employment of interpretive methods will not only increase diversity in research, but also increase coherence between the research question and method selected. Though no single method cuts across all the different types of research and aims within the psychology of religion, and no single method is privileged (Belzen & Hood, 2006), there is a postpositivist leaning trend in current psychology of religion studies, as evidenced by selected research paradigms and methods. However, there appears to be a growing interpretive influence.

Transparency, research question, and rationale were assessed in each article to answer the third question regarding fit. There was a large inconsistency in the standard of quality across the articles. Transparency, overall, was modest and varied, with 44.07% offering good transparency. This variation suggested different levels of assumptions held by researchers about communicating research details, with some offering rigorous reporting methods with step-by-step transparency and others merely naming the method with a citation. Fit was difficult to discern in the latter cluster of articles. Though transparency is an important standard for qualitative inquiry due to the diversity of methods, sometimes the methodological rigor revealed a positivist influence. Some studies meticulously outlined the methods but were reductive in discussing the findings. For instance, some studies offered good transparency on their research methods and procedures but merely listed participant answers without interpreting them (e.g., Dahl et al., 2010). Other studies reduced their data to code books (e.g., Sherman et al., 2018) or word frequencies (e.g., Snook et al., 2019) without offering further analyses.

Further, there was a surprising trend of understating the research question: 37.85% explicitly stated their research question and 62.15% did not. Because the research question describes the purpose and focus of the investigation, its lack hinders the clarity of the researcher's goals. On the other hand, 15% of the articles stated a hypothesis although the goal of qualitative research is not predictability and generalization. Additionally, only a little over a quarter of the articles (27.68%) gave a rationale for why qualitative inquiry and/or the specific qualitative method selected was a good fit for exploring their research question.

Due to a combination of these factors, fit was difficult to determine for 27.12% of the articles. Yet, for the articles in which fit could be determined, there were slightly more articles that had low fit (38.98%) than high fit (33.90%). Studies often sought in-depth, thick explanations for understanding experiences in their research question/purpose but utilized deductive and/or reductive research methods. Also, many studies that sought to confirm a hypothesis or apply a priori categories could have achieved research goals through quantitative means (e.g., a survey), which would have been a less time-consuming process than an in-depth qualitative approach. Nevertheless, the 33.90% of studies with a good fit reveal a positive trend for qualitative inquiry. Among those articles with good fit ($N = 60$), 75% of them were from an interpretive-constructivist paradigm ($N = 45$) and only 23.33% of them were from a postpositivist paradigm ($N = 14$), which underlines the ability of inductive, in-depth methods to answer complex, nuanced research questions and purposes explored by qualitative inquiry.

These elements contribute to the final question of the in-depth investigation of religion/spirituality and culture in the articles. Belzen and Hood (2006) have proposed that "the ideal task" for those in the field of psychology of religion is "to provide additional knowledge about religion from a psychological perspective" (p. 7) and have thus recommended that the field might "benefit from a stronger orientation toward the hermeneutical tradition" (p. 8). Qualitative inquiry offers the unique ability to explore the complexity of religious/spiritual and cultural experience, especially in how they are connected. Yet, only about a quarter of the articles (26.55%) offered an in-depth study on religion and only 15.82% on culture. It was expected that a majority of the articles would provide an exploration of religion at some level (58.76%), but it was unanticipated that 14.69% of the articles would not at all. Similarly, for the treatment of cultural components, an overwhelming majority of 74.58% made no mention of it, while 8.47% offered some.

In light of these statistics, we characterized the lack of exploration of religion/spirituality and culture as missed opportunities. The studies demonstrated great potential for rich exploration of religion/spirituality and cultural nuances, yet this was often overlooked. First, there were two major barriers to an in-depth study of religion: (1) reductive methodology, and (2) the lack of exploration into psychic functioning of religious/spiritual phenomena (Belzen & Hood, 2006). In methodology, reducing meaning-laden transcripts to word frequencies cannot capture the intricate processes of religious/

spiritual experience. This is also the case for deductive methods that do not allow new meanings to emerge and merely test predetermined theories. The second barrier was that articles often addressed an issue (e.g., marital conflict, disaster relief) in a religious setting (e.g., church, clergy, clergy couple), but did not address the psychic religious and/or spiritual experience of these issues at a deeper level. For instance, a study about interchurch couples (Williams & Lawler, 1998) and a study about interpersonal conflict between clergy within a Southern Baptist church (Breen, 2008) both missed the opportunity to examine the psychic dimensions of a religious/spiritual experience by focusing only on the experience of conflict apart from religious/spiritual issues (also the case in Berry et al., 2012).

Knowledge is context bound (Pak, 2017; Polkinghorne, 1983), but studies often limited the context only to religion, leading to an inadequate addressing of the complexities and multiplicities of the cultures that the human psyche is embedded in. A large majority of articles did not even identify cultural components (e.g., ethnic culture, gender, country of origin) that could influence the religious experience of the participants. This is similar to a previous review by Arnett (2008), which found that even when studies were conducted outside of the United States, cultural context and background were rarely mentioned—much like all the studies conducted within the U.S. that did not address culture—likely with the assumption of generalization that culture did not matter. It is also consistent with previous review findings that there seems to be little to no relationship between cultural psychology and psychology of religion (Belzen, 2010). The opportunity to examine culture felt especially missed when the study was conducted in a culture-specific context (e.g., in a specific demographic population, different country/countries) but did not incorporate cultural considerations in its analysis, interpretation, and discussion. For instance, in a study about the attitudes of African American clergy responding to postvention needs of suicide survivors, there was a missed opportunity to incorporate cultural and social components unique to the African American community that impacts those attitudes (Crenshaw, 2015; see also Keefe et al., 2016; Himelhoch & Njie-Carr, 2016). Another study that compared children's understanding of religion among Arab-Muslims, Asian-Muslims, Christians, and Hindus also did not consider the cultural factors that may have contributed to the differences among these populations (Takriti et al., 2006).

Finally, religion and culture are deeply connected, yet a majority of the articles reviewed did not assume that they were. Only 9.04% ($N = 16$) of the articles addressed both religion/spirituality and culture in-depth, which indicates that 90.40% do not. Even in exemplary studies, in terms of qualitative methods and investigation of religion/spirituality, this complexity was not always addressed. One example is a study conducted by Silverman and colleagues (2016) on Jewish beliefs about God. Though the religious elements were explored with in-depth interpretations, it did not account for how the Jewish identity is both a religion and an ethnic culture. Thus, it missed the opportunity to gain even further insight by applying the nuance of the religious ethnic dynamics of being Jewish to the interviews, analysis, and interpretations. In the articles that did offer in-depth exploration of religious/spiritual experience and of culture, some exemplar studies emerged that employed the strengths of qualitative inquiry to illuminate nuances. Example research articles are discussed below to highlight these features.

3.5.2 Example Qualitative Studies

The first set of articles present rich insight into religious experience. First, Williamson and colleagues (2000) demonstrated an in-depth investigation of the meaning of the practice of serpent handling within the context of the Holiness-Pentecostal sect, and specifically the Serpent Handling Sect (SHS), through robust research quality. Phenomenological, hermeneutical, and thematic analyses were employed to conduct an inductive, interpretive analysis of the religious/spiritual experience of "taking up a snake" based on a literal interpretation of Mark 16:17–18, offered with the rationale that a phenomenological method allows for participants' meanings of experiences to emerge. These methods were well suited "to describe the personal experience of the anointing" (Williamson et al., 2000, p. 224) through their own narrative of the experience (p. 225), which could not be drawn from surveys. Researcher bracketing and hermeneutic interpretations allowed the study to make "religious sense" (p. 238) of the participants' personal experiences in response to the more "scientific" research conducted thus far on SHS. Therefore, Williamson and colleagues have successfully conducted an in-depth analysis of the phenomenological experience of serpent handlers, revealing their belief that this experience was sourced from anointing and, to a lesser degree, faith. These findings were beyond what could have been produced by measures or surveys and have the benefit of hermeneutic interpretation for fresh insight.

Additionally, as alluded to previously, Silverman and colleagues (2016) presented an in-depth study of Jewish belief and representation of God. Using mixed methods, they sought to draw out unique cultural nuances before applying the findings to a quantitative study comparing representations of God across religions. Acknowledging the inadequacy of surveys to capture the complexity of Jewish beliefs about God, they began with an ethnographic study that included two years of field observation and interviews with 29 participants. To allow participants' own interpretations and experiences of Jewish prayers and Jewish life to emerge, they paid careful attention to the "meanings and experiences of the bodily sensations of both the anthropologists and interviewee" within their context (p. 121), thereby conducting analysis beyond the surface level into the nonverbal and cultural context. They also sought to examine relationships among belief, practice, and the syncretic views that Jews hold, a nuance that cannot be drawn from surveys alone, which led to the surprising discovery that some Jews thought of God as a universal or cosmic force. The findings reveal that Jews were likely to believe in the existence of God but held diverse representations of God (e.g., relational, ineffable, universal). The second quantitative study followed up on these findings to compare Jews to other religious groups, yielding findings that Jewish representations were unstable and indefinite compared to those of other religious groups; the content of these representations were investigated through the qualitative study. In this way, both qualitative and quantitative studies were carried out separately and findings were well integrated.

In another study, Russo-Netzer (2018) used qualitative inquiry to investigate spirituality outside of institutionalized religion. The in-depth, semi-structured interviews with phenomenological analysis used in this study were well suited to explore deep spiritual change. The interviews were designed with researcher bracketing and open-ended questions to enable participants' subjective experiences to emerge, and analysis was done through an immersive, iterative process that analyzed meaning units rather than a mere coding of words. These methods yielded thick descriptions of internal-personal and external-environmental resources utilized by Israelis during spiritual change outside of institutionalized religion. As a result, they proposed an overarching theory with the themes that emerged. Present in all participant interviews regarding outside-institution spirituality was a search for real spirituality (Amiti in Hebrew) due to the multiplicity of options in the "spiritual marketplace" (p. 3). They discerned authenticity through spiritual touchstones that were other-oriented (open to questioning as opposed to dogmatic authority; staying connected to ordinary experience of the world rather than secluding) and self-oriented (bodily experience; signs providing guidance). This study demonstrated a strong understanding of the unique contributions of qualitative research: the researcher did not apologize for the "narrow" focus of the study and rather suggested future research in other populations in order to gain cross-cultural insight. Thus, this article offered insight into the nuanced and complex world of spirituality outside of religion for Israelis.

The following articles go even more in-depth by locating religious experience within its cultural milieu to extract further insight. Building on studies that have found that Tibetans have low psychological distress despite experiencing traumatic events due to religious coping and protective factors, Hussain and Bhushan (2011) employed an interpretive approach to unearth emic, cultural coping resources. Specifically, the religious and cultural impacts of Tibetan Buddhism, or Lamaism, on coping were explored in 12 Tibetan refugees. IPA (Smith, 1996) conducted on narrative case studies proved to be a good fit to extract culturally derived resources, as it allowed researchers to capture personal experience in detail to determine how meanings were constructed by individuals. By doing so, they gained insight into unique practices and resources: the protective hand of the Dalai Lama and other Lamas, Buddhist philosophy and practices, community bonding and support, and historical exemplars of strength and resiliency. Thus, the article highlighted that religious experiences are embedded in culture, while simultaneously showing how cultural coping strategies are influenced by religious values. These dimensions could not have been captured through deductive methods, and considerations of the cultural context of the religion through an in-depth interpretive method allowed for new insight into the religious resources of Tibetan Buddhist refugees. Future utilization of these methods will be instrumental in capturing complex, culturally-embedded religious experiences and meanings.

Kim and Pak (2013) have presented an example of utilizing in-depth narrative analysis with multiple case study design to examine the spiritual development of five Korean immigrant women in their midlives, through which they offer rich insight into religion/spirituality and culture. Understanding that "theoretical models birthed in Western societies do not adequately address collectivistic interpretations of spiritual maturity among Koreans" (Kim & Pak, 2013, p. 4) and the increasing complexity introduced in the dual cultural context of Korean-immigrant Christians, the researchers sought to investigate and integrate the two cultural views of spiritual maturity to gain a holistic understanding of relationship with God and others. The case-study method with narrative analysis was an instrumental research method to accomplish this goal, as it allowed for the investigation of "the multiplicity and complexity of issues embedded in a woman's unique spiritual journey as a bi-cultural Christian" (pp. 7–8). Utilizing McAdam's (1993) life story method for the interview allowed participants to articulate their stories across their lifetimes. Synthesis and interpretation through both within-case and cross-case analysis aided in producing thick descriptions of the experiences, which provided deeper knowledge of the intersectionality of the participants. The within-case analysis provided insight into the conflicting cultural values within a person in their spiritual journey and the cross-case analysis allowed for commonalities and distinctions to be drawn. Overall, the article accentuated the strengths of qualitative inquiry and the unique contribution it can make to illuminate the intricate nuances at the intersection of multiple cultures and religion and the limitations of current models in understanding spiritual maturity.

Finally, with the knowledge of indigenous healing practices' capacity to produce richer healing experiences for trauma than traditional trauma counseling informed by the importation of the notion of Post-Traumatic Stress Disorder (PTSD) developed largely from North America and Europe (Watters, 2011), Ting (2016) utilized a case-study approach to illuminate the religious contributions to resiliency within Yushu Tibetan survivors following the 2010 earthquake in Qinghai, China. Imported trauma therapy models (e.g., systematized, diagnosis, exposure therapy) were detrimental to the healing of survivors following the Sichuan earthquake in 2008 because they overly pathologized and overlooked post-traumatic growth in China. Thus, the study sought to integrate unique nuances of Yushu religion and culture (e.g., reliance on folk healers, herbal medicine, and religious leaders and practices for healing; Buddhist conceptualization of suffering; familism) in investigating their resiliency. An ethnographic method within a hermeneutic anthropological approach was employed to observe the society from the participants' perspectives and to allow for their unique experience to emerge. Furthermore, a case study approach was used, informed by the author's immersive, year-long fieldwork. The inductive, interpretive approach was a good fit for their aim to study the resilience of this population. Analysis revealed that the Yushu Tibetans had an open-hearted attitude towards life and death, which the author indicates should not be mistaken for psychoanalytic conceptualizations of repression or defensiveness. These findings provide rich implications for a new paradigm of psychological care that integrates religion as a result of the thick descriptions of religious experience in resiliency and highlights the urgency for research that provides in-depth exploration of culture and religion.

3.5.3 Conclusion

One could gather from these findings that a positivist influence on qualitative inquiry in the psychology of religion has truncated a more in-depth exploration of religious/spiritual and cultural issues. In efforts to make findings generalizable, data was often reduced, which removed the nuances of how culture may be impacting a religious experience, even within culture-specific studies. Ponterotto (2005) has identified this risk of "postpositivizing" (p. 127) interpretive-constructivist qualitative inquiry and the tendency to adopt qualitative methods without a firm understanding of the philosophical paradigms that undergird them. Our findings have confirmed major critiques of the natural science bias in psychology of religion (Pak, 2017), even amongst the small percentage of qualitative studies.

The utilization of in-depth qualitative methods has wide implications in psychology and religion. As revealed through the work of Williamson and colleagues (2000) on serpent handlers, utilization of interpretive methods enables the mining of fresh insight into religious/cultural experiences that cannot be obtained through quantitative means. This was similarly the case for Silverman and colleagues' (2016) study on Jewish belief and perceptions of God and Russo-Netzer's (2018) study of Israelis' spiritual experiences outside of religion. This in-depth exploration is taken even further by embedding the religious experience in its cultural context. Hussain and Bhushan (2011) have revealed the unique religious, cultural coping mechanisms of Tibetan Buddhists through inductive means. Yet, the urgency of culturally embedded understanding of religion and spirituality is also rooted in the unhelpful, and sometimes harmful, effects of assuming a generalized, etic understanding of religious/spiritual issues of psychology. While Kim and Pak (2013) have illuminated and addressed the limitations of applying only concepts developed from North America and Europe to understanding spiritual maturity in bicultural Korean-immigrant Christian women, Ting (2016) highlighted the harmful effects of asserting imported constructs of PTSD and expectations of trauma therapy to those recovering from the 2008 earthquake in China. Overall, these sample qualitative studies present a hopeful direction for psychology and religion studies to illuminate the inseparable nature of religion/spirituality and culture that a human psyche is embedded in. Through their common interpretive framework, they have extracted ideographic, emic knowledge to draw fresh insight into human experience, and this insight has provided means to better assist people in understanding unique religious experiences and culture-specific psychology.

4 Cultural Psychology, Religion, and Narrative Inquiry

Because modern psychology has emerged in the past hundred years in primarily Western industrialized countries, the field largely reflects the values of North America and Europe (Arnett, 2008; Lawson et al., 2007). Thus, psychology is indigenous to a Western context (Dueck, 2007). Because the values of

Western psychology are used to describe, theorize, evaluate, and research individuals whose way of life may be different, ethnocentricity (i.e., a cultural bias where one's own culture is believed to have the only true or sufficient understanding of the world) is a critical problem in psychology. In order to study the phenomena at hand, it is important not to impose one's own categories and assumptions. However, it is impossible to know the other without using our own understanding according to our own categories. Although we can never escape a perspectival understanding on any subject, we frequently assume cultural beliefs are universal truths.

Recognizing the value-laden cultural shortcomings of psychology originating from North America and Europe, cultural and indigenous psychologies have developed to respond to growing global, political, economic, religious, and social needs in various parts of the world. The damaging impact of Western (largely American) psychology in developing countries has been well articulated by numerous authors (Dueck & Reimer, 2009; Lawson, Graham, & Baker, 2007; Sinha & Holtzman, 1984). Building culturally robust and intelligible theories capable of more effectively and sensitively responding to complex problems faced by a rapidly changing world, calls for openness to diverse orientations in knowledge as well as empirical approach to psychological inquiry. As outlined by Gergen, Josselson, and Freeman (2015), qualitative inquiry holds much promise to enrich the discipline by inspiring interdisciplinary collaboration and minority inclusion that leads to new understanding, theory building, and social change.

4.1 *Psychology and Culture*

It has been nearly seventy years since Kroeber and Kluckhohn (1952) published their seminal book, which included a list of over 200 different definitions of culture and described culture as "the most central problem of all social sciences" (p. 3). However, psychology as a discipline still has not reached any agreement on a coherent definition or concept of culture even with all the recent emphasis on multiculturalism and diversity in American psychology (e.g., APA, 2002; APA, 2009). The major approaches to studying the relationship between culture and psychology are cultural psychology, cross-cultural psychology, and indigenous psychology; however, they developed largely independently from each other, which has contributed to some confusion in the field. Although these diverse ways of thinking through culture and psychology are merging, Ratner (2008a) warns that the fundamental differences between positivist objectivity and the original, holistic concept of culture and dialectical philosophy (e.g., Meacham, 1999; Riegel,1976) underlying cultural psychology cannot be eclectically combined and homogenized. The meaning-structures of culture and culturally mediated actions on cognitions, emotions, and motivations not only require psychology to reassess its object, but also its methodology (Belzen, 2001; Ratner, 2008b; Straub & Weidemann, 2006).

Historically, *cross-cultural psychology* has developed primarily in the U.S. over the last fifty years. It focused on testing and applying Western psychological theories and measures with people outside of North America and Europe in search of empirically valid psychological universals (Straub &Weidermann, 2006). Grounded in the positivist paradigm, cross-cultural psychologists treat culture as simple, discrete, overt variables that transcend time and place, where a broad set of shared differences can be reduced quantitatively and compared across societies (Ratner, 2008a). Although cross-cultural psychology tries to attend to cultural factors, its retention of positivist methodology in measuring and testing theories primarily developed in the U.S. has been criticized frequently for distorting the cultural origins and characteristics of psychological phenomena (Ratner & Hui, 2003; Ratner, 1997).

Indigenous psychology, on the other hand, developed since the 1970s as a reaction to modern, scientific Western psychology being transplanted to non-Western cultural contexts (Allwood, 2002; Heelas & Lock, 1981). Similar to cross-cultural and cultural psychology, indigenous psychology is not a single discipline but loosely integrated heterogeneous groups with internal contradictions and contestations on diverse theoretical and methodological issues (see Ratner, 2008a; Yang, 2012 for a discussion on indigenous and indigenized psychology). Because psychology originating from North America and Europe was introduced in many countries during the colonial period, the indigenizing process of psychologies was often perceived as a part of postcolonial movement by researchers in efforts to develop psychologies that were rooted in their own local cultural traditions (Berry et al., 1997; Sinha, 1997; Sinha & Holtzman, 1984). Indigenous psychology scholars denounced existing psychological theories for not being universal but culture-blind and culture-bound in overlooking their own particular indigeneity and implicit assumptions. Thus, indigenous psychology not only opposes a positivist view of science as objective and neutral, but also scrutinizes mainstream psychology as Euro-American centric in its dependence on the social and cultural conditions in which it was produced (Allwood, 2002; Allwood & Berry, 2006; Kim, Yang, & Hwang, 2006). Whereas indigenous psychology is anchored in the specific local cultural context, one important aspiration of the movement, similar to cross-cultural psychology, is to compare indigenous psychology from different societies and use the emerging concepts and overall patterns to integrate and achieve a truly universal, pan-human psychology (Allwood & Berry, 2006; Berry & Kim, 1993).

As the term Völkerpsychologie was first coined by Wilhelm Humboldt and subsequently used by Wundt over 150 years ago, Ratner (2008a, 2012) explains *cultural psychology* was originally conceived as "macro-cultural psychology" in that the structure of culture (e.g., social institutions, artifacts, cultural concepts) is understood to reciprocally form and maintain higher mental functions (e.g., self, perception, emotion, cognition, motivation). In other words, culture does not simply interact with or influence psychology; instead, culture and psychology are inseparable just like two sides of a coin. According to Shweder (1990),

> Cultural psychology is the study of the way cultural traditions and social practices regulate, express, transform, and permute the human psyche, resulting less in psychic unity for humankind than in ethnic divergences in mind, self and emotion. Cultural psychology is the study of the ways subject and object, self and other, psyche and culture, person and context, figure and ground, practitioner and practice live together, require each other, and, dynamically, dialectically, and jointly make each other up. (p. 1)

Ultimately, this locates cultural psychology as an interpretive discipline stressing the importance of context for meaning (Belzen, 2001; Browning, 2001; Rater, 2008a; Shweder, 1991; Straub & Weidemann, 2006). While mainstream psychology overemphasizes intra-individual processes, Belzen (2001) explains,

> cultural psychology does not search inside the human being to investigate belief, feeling, reasoning and behavior, but rather tries to understand how the specific "form of life" the person is embedded in constitutes and constructs feelings, thoughts and conduct. (p. 47)

In this way, cultural psychologists conceive culture psychologically as a meaning-structed "hermeneutic concept" and view human behavior to be meaningful only when interpreted in the social-cultural context, which takes into account environment, history, culture, and complexity of real-life activity (Straub & Weidemann, 2006; for overview on cultural psychology see Cole, 1996; Shweder, 1991). Unlike cross-cultural psychology, cultural psychology does not treat culture as an independent variable but as an interpretive concept; rather than focusing on measuring *behavior* (stimulus-response), it conceives of culture on a different level by studying *action* (situated) (Rater, 2008a).

Following the cultural-historical Russian tradition, Vygotsky (1978) elaborated on the activity theory in the early 1900s to bridge the gap between the individual subject and social reality. He identified three cultural factors which organized psychic functioning: (1) activities (e.g., producing goods, raising children, education), (2) artifacts (e.g., tools, books, technology), and (3) concepts about things and people (e.g., law, religion, customs, social structures). Although psychological development dynamically depended on all three cultural factors, Vygotsky stressed the dominance of activities over the other two in structuring higher mental functions, which "represent a cast of collective social relations between people" and "a transfer into the personality of an inward relation of a social order that constitutes the basis of the social structure of the human personality" (pp. 169–190). It is important to note that action not only situates the context in a holistic sense (i.e., recognizes the lack of distinction between mental, moral, spiritual, and physical), but also contains the notion of goals, purpose, and intention. It requires an organizing principle that is faithful to the complexities observed when people engage in intentional performances to realize their often unarticulated goals.

Thus, deeply rooted in cultural-historical, dialectical, and hermeneutic philosophy, cultural psychology has continued to develop in Germany, Russia, U.S., and other countries over the years. While the foundational ideas that culture and psychological factors are mutually constitutive and interdependent (i.e., culture contains psychological phenomena and psychological phenomena forms and embodies cultural practices) are accepted by many cultural psychologists, Rater (2008a, 2012) raises concern that the original macro emphasis in cultural psychology has more recently been displaced by micro level focusing on individual and interpersonal notions of culture (for discussion on diverse approaches in cultural psychology see Ratner, 1999). He warns that this is a huge problem and blind spot in psychology in that the macro cultural factors are ultimately political, and history reveals different elite interest groups with power have always dominated and controlled the mass with various cultural artifacts and tools (cf. Chibber, 2013). Ratner (2008a) cautions, however, while attempting to oppose and free from Western domination, indigenous psychologists often fall into the trap of nationalistic identity politics, which privileges cultural insiders and glorify the group's self-definition without critically examining oppressive cultural artifacts or exploitative power relations within the system (also see Chibber, 2013). For this reason, the cultural origins, characteristics, politics, and psychological function of phenomena all need to be rigorously analyzed. Though contributions from indigenous and cross-cultural psychology could fill in gaps, Ratner suggests cultural psychology provides the most comprehensive foundational paradigm for fully apprehending the relationship between culture and psychology and should serve as the organizing framework as the discipline continues to evolve and work towards coherence and being unified.

4.2 *Macro Culture, Religion, and Psychological Phenomena*

Based on Vygotsky's (1978) cultural-historical theory, macro cultural psychology emphasizes that psychological phenomena, particularly higher mental functions (e.g., consciousness, intention, meaning), is a subjective manifestation of cultural activity and the product of historical development (e.g., wars, immigration, technology, family, religious beliefs); in other words, psychology is not independent but is derived from the social form of collective life (Ratner, 2012). Because psychology traditionally focused heavily on intra-individual and interpersonal processes, it has largely neglected the cultural or macro level impact on human development. For this reason, it is beneficial to become more cognizant of how macro aspects of culture, such as social class, religion, institutions, and communal/organizational practices, dialectically and historically form psychological phenomena. While it is not possible to discuss all these issues in the scope of this paper, scholars from cultural, indigenous, and liberation psychology have made insightful contributions in this area, which could be good resources for readers interested in psychological and religious perspectives from diverse countries around the world such as Africa, India, China, Philippine, and Latin America (e.g., Comas-Diaz & Riveras, 2020; Dueck & Reimer, 1998; Enriquez, 1994; Fanon, 1967; Haque, 2004; Kim, Yang, & Hwang, 2006; Ndlovu-Gatsheni, 2013; Rao, Paranjpe, & Dalal, 2008). To illustrate how people's lives are structured by traditional systems of thought and how their psychological needs are historically met through various religious practices, an example of Korea's complex tapestry of religious heritage will be discussed below.

4.2.1 Traditional Religious Practices and Psychological Function: Example of Korea

To understand the dialectical relationship between cultural-historical phenomena and psychological function, one can look at the roots of Eastern psychological thinking, which go back over two millennia and are entangled in the systems of religious thoughts such as Confucianism and Taoism (Ho, 1988; Sinha, 1997; Allwood & Berry, 2006; Sundararajan, 2015; Pak, in press). These traditional teachings and religious practices reflected shared normative ideals of social, political, and familial hierarchy. They also played a powerful role in people's lives by implicitly providing fundamental relational models of social life and a context to process emotion and cope with various challenges in life (Sundararajan, 2015; Pak, 2006). In this way, religion contributed not only to core ideals, but also implicitly met psychological needs that became interwoven and essential to everyday life.

In addition to Confucianism and Taoism, in the Korean context, Shamanism is also thought to be an enduring core religious worldview underlying Korean people's mindset and cultural practices (Baker, 2008). For this reason, amongst diverse imported religions in Korea, Christianity particularly struggled with assimilation of Shamanistic elements, such as emphasis on material blessings and healing ministry (Kim, 1999; Kim, 2006). Historically, this resulted in the division of Korean Protestant Christianity into two major camps: (1) the "paternal/Confucianistic" mainline traditions fundamentally stressing accuracy of doctrine and Scripture, and (2) the "maternal/Shamanistic" Pentecostal and *minjung* emphasizing healing and blessing for the poor and oppressed (Ryu, 2000; Kim, 2006). Putting aside theological issues, which is outside of the scope of this paper, most recent neuroscience findings not only suggest that emotion (conscious/explicit) and affect (unconscious/implicit) are inseparable, but also that both are needed to function properly. Since ancient times, religion (e.g., mythology, Shamanism, Animism) was utilized to control the unconscious and integrate it with the conscious mind at an individual and collective level (Winkelman, 2004; d'Aquili & Newberg, 1999).

In this way, religion functioned as one of the most effective ways to cope with the various challenges of life. With a long history of invasions and oppression, the Korean people endured *han*, a term used to describe the depths of human suffering (Park, 1993). Ordinary people's *han* was traditionally healed by Shamanism, the country's oldest folk religion, through rituals. More recently this emotional function of releasing *han* has been shared by Pentecostal churches, which has arguably contributed to Pentecostalism's rapid growth in Korea (Kim, 2006). One unique form of indigenous Korean spiritual practice involves *tong-sung-ki-do*, which is praying in unison or crying out loud together corporately. This style of prayer is not only considered an important part of the spirit-filled prayer life amongst Korean Pentecostal Christians as a fervent and earnest way of crying out to God, but is also thought to have a strong connection with releasing Korean people's *han*—unresolved resentment, bitterness, emotional pain, or suffering (Kim, 1999).

Thus, the socially, politically, and economically oppressed Korean people were particularly drawn to God, who they believed would grant them material happiness, liberation from suffering, and a better alternative to their current reality (Yun, 2010; Pak, 2020). In the case of Korea, rather than clashing, culture and religion are often intertwined and can be mutually reinforcing. It is difficult and almost impossible to separate religious conversion from the indigenous understanding of spirituality. To an extent, indigenization is also arguably a necessary precursor when it comes to enabling a receptive environment for new imported religion. For many scholars, the "Koreanization" of Christianity is the reason why the faith was so well-received in comparison to other countries (e.g., Grayson, 2006; Lee, 2006). More specifically, Christianity was able to take root and transition fluidly as Protestantism incorporated Korean tradition into its practice. Christianity spread in Korea because it was able to coexist in harmony with Korea's indigenous religious beliefs and practices and met people's challenging needs living in contemporary society.

4.2.2 Modern "Scientific" View: Example of Emotion and Religious Experience

In the West (particularly in the American academic mainstream), on the other hand, the process of making psychology pursue abstract universal laws resulted in eliminating central human functions, such as consciousness, intention, meaning, as well as religion. Because the natural science paradigm only permitted a narrow range of phenomena to be studied, researchers were denied the possibility of studying the rich mental phenomena people experience everyday (O'Neill, 2002). One area in particular that deserves closer attention is the "scientific" understanding of emotion and religious experience (Pak, 2020).

Today, scholars agree that religious experience has an emotional component (e.g., Norris, 2005; Roberts 2007); however, as Azari and Birnbacherm (2004) point out, the historical over-simplification of emotion has dominated research on the role of emotion in religious experience due to two major theories in Western psychology: (1) the noncognitive/somatic view (e.g., James-Lange, 1884/5) that believes emotion consists of a pure, automatic, prewired, bodily state of arousal that comes before and apart from any thoughts and beliefs; and (2) the cognitive/appraisal approach (e.g., Schachter & Singer, 1962) that argues even if bodily arousal is involved, the specificity of emotion is given by some kind of cognitive appraisal. The simple conceptualization of emotion as a pure bodily arousal (feeling) or a pure cognitive construction (thinking) has not been supported by research (Azari & Birnbacher, 2004; d'Aquili & Newberg, 1999).

Empirical evidence has challenged both reductive models of emotion and demonstrated that emotion is better conceived as neither pure bodily arousal nor pure cognitive process but engages both (Rolls, 1999). Current neuroscientific findings indicate dynamic interactions between the cognitive, affective, motivational, bodily arousal, and transformational components (LeDoux, 1996; Rolls, 1999) and integrative understanding of feelings and belief is supported by contemporary studies in this area (Roberts, 2007; Azari & Birnbachler, 2004; Norris, 2005). In fact, recent psychological research on emotion shows the complex interdependence between cognition regulating emotion and emotion regulating cognition (Clore, 2011). One study (Mar et al., 2006) illustrates how emotion organizes action by stimulating conscious thought and permitting a revision of beliefs and intentions. For example, the emotions from a drama or movie seem to help regulate thought by drawing our attention to the important aspects of situations. They also facilitate learning through the vicarious feeling of emotions rather than the venting of emotions as previously thought. Thus, it appears emotion actually helps people think much more than they would without it. Gross' (2001) research, on the other hand, demonstrates that the role of cognition is to shape emotion as it develops rather than to suppress it later. He found people could more easily change or dampen emotions by reinterpreting events than suppressing emotions which was harder and reduced people's ability to remember.

Therefore, current findings suggest that cognition exerts control over emotion, not by conflict or suppression, but by shaping, situating, contextualizing, and changing its meaning (Clore, 2011). One implication Clore points out is that the power of affect depends on how cognition constrains its meaning; more specifically, cognition appears to shape low-level, affective reactions into more precise emotions (e.g., sadness, fear, anger, shame). Other findings, however, indicate that primary emotion at the subcortical level exerts stronger control on higher cognitive function, which explains why deep emotional experience is not always in full awareness to be consciously or explicitly regulated through cognition (Panksepp, 1998). Recent evidence from neuroscience research supports that belief in supernatural beings or the spirit world involves an innate human mind, which involves a higher psychological process to organize and make sense of emotional experience through a religiously and culturally mediated meaning system (Hewitt, 2012; Lewis-Williams, 2010; Azari & Birnbachler, 2004; Panksepp, 1998). Hewitt describes, for example, how altered states of consciousness or trance experienced by shamans since ancient times contributed to the development of religion all over the world as people sought ways to harmoniously exist in connection with nature and the cosmos.

In other words, just as emotional experience is a complex matter involving thinking and feeling (Damasio, 1999), religious experience cannot be reduced to pure feeling or thought (Roberts, 2007; Azari & Birnbachler, 2004; Norris, 2005). Insights drawn from brain imaging studies show that religious and mystical experiences are mediated by complex patterns of neural activity; they involve the autonomic nervous system, the limbic system, and neocortical areas. Religious experience cannot be located to a specific brain region, according to d'Aquili and Newberg (1999). However, they argue religion has not disappeared since ancient periods because the basic aspects of religion are hardwired in the brain and help human survival and adaptability through self-maintenance and self-transcendence, which are used in most cultures to gain a sense of control over an unpredictable world.

Winkelman (2004) similarly explains that Shamanism and Animism involve innate emotional preverbal brain structures that utilize integrative altered states of consciousness to facilitate a sense of connection and oneness to self, others, and the world, which promotes social adaptation, community integration, personal development, and healing. Winkelman believes Shamanistic and Animistic principles embodied in spirits are used to manipulate unconscious aspects of self. This helps unite the unconscious mind with the conscious mind, which is mediated by language and the cultural system, to give order and situate the person in the world. In this way, religious traditions provide emotionally charged cultural symbols through rituals to integrate the psychological, spiritual, and somatic spheres and promote healing in the community.

Brahinsky (2018), however, points out that both neuroscience and cultural studies are currently divided by two different views on emotion and affect: (1) separating emotions thought to be mediated by reason/language from prelinguistic affect charged with energy, and (2) not dividing affect and emotion into different physiological regions because they are *both* pervasive dimensions of brain activity and deeply entangled with the external context. This means that it is not practically possible to tease apart linguistically controlled emotion from unconstrained affect. What appears to be conscious thought is controlled by unconscious or implicit affective processes. Interestingly, Brahinsky describes what is commonly observed in Pentecostal spiritual practice (e.g., explosive emotional rupture, trance states, praying in tongues) may be perceived as irrational and impulsive; however, he argues these spiritual practices initially involve the conscious learning and cultivation of complex skills, which become automatic and spontaneous when repeated over time.

Thus, a much more complex picture of emotion has emerged, suggesting emotion is tightly bound up with cognition (Russell, 2003; Lazarus, 1982) and culture (Joshanloo, 2019; Sundararajan, 2015; Markus & Kitayama, 1991). Current studies suggest there may be basic emotions at the bodily level, but most emotions are cognitively mediated by the social and cultural context in such a way that it is not practical to conceive of them separately; emotion dynamically involves both cognitive and noncognitive processes (Sundararajan, 2005;

Hwang & Huang, 2012). In other words, if recent research and theory on emotion (e.g., Russell, 2003; Lazarus, 1982) is to be taken seriously, an accurate account of religious experience calls for a deeper understanding and integration of embodied thinking and feeling (d'Aquili & Newberg, 1999; Sundararajan, 2015).

Recent advances in cognitive science (e.g., Damasio, 1999; LeDoux, 1996; Rolls, 1999; Russell, 2003) as well as scholarly contributions from diverse cultural and religious perspectives (e.g., Sundararajan, 2005; Hwang & Huang, 2012) have deepened our understanding of religious experience. The previous example of Korea shows that religious experience cannot be reduced to an overly simplistic account of emotion or cognitivity, just as emotional experience is a complex matter of both thinking and feeling.

4.3 *Culture, Religion, and Qualitative Methodology*

In spite of the process of rapid globalization and migration, religion is intimately bound with cultural tradition especially in the non-Western world as demonstrated in the example of Korea. For this reason, not only can religion and culture not be ignored, but also a different kind of research is required than what is commonly practiced in mainstream psychology, in general, and psychology of religion, in particular (Belzen, 2001; Ratner, 2008, 2012). As Belzen (2001) states, religion is primarily a cultural phenomenon and the particular cultural and religious "form of life" cannot be discarded if psychology hopes to be relevant. For the last two decades, cultural psychologists (e.g., Belzen, 2010; Cole, 1996; Ratner, 2008) have identified the problems in utilizing methods developed out of the natural sciences to compare people across cultures and search for invariable psychic structures. Two major problems have wide consensus among cultural and indigenous psychologists: (1) overly focusing on the diffusion of a Western theory of self or individual construal (Marcus & Kitayama, 1991; Heelas & Lock, 1981), and (2) the tremendous resources invested in importing, adapting, and normalizing Western measures, largely due to blindly following the positivist-empiricist notions of science (Ratner & Hui, 2003; Ratner, 1997).

Because psychology is dominated by positivism, Ponterotto (2002) stresses the need for more qualitative research utilizing constructivist and critical theory paradigms, which show greater sensitivity to previously excluded populations and understanding of their experiences in the context of indigenous values and traditions. Thus, qualitative research methods have become central in indigenous and cultural psychology, which strongly advocate for the development of ethical obligations, methodological pluralism, and human science approaches to extend the scientific rigor and psychological knowledge (Allwood & Berry, 2006; Kim, Yang, & Hwang, 2006; Ponterotto, 2002; Wertz,

2011). In subfields such as multiculturalism, the growing momentum toward qualitative research has been recognized as "the fifth force" by some scholars who believe it "will have as great an impact on the field of psychology as have had the four previous forces of psychoanalysis, behaviorism, humanism, and feminism/multiculturalism" (Ponterotto, Costa, & Werner-Lin, 2002, p. 413).

While cross-cultural psychology espouses positivist methodology, an important aspect of cultural psychology is recognition of qualitative methodology; however, Ratner (2008b) points out that cultural psychology is diverse theoretically and that a qualitative approach is utilized differently depending on which ontological and epistemological assumptions are adhered to explicitly or implicitly. As a way to map the complex array, he suggests not only differentiating cultural psychology theory on two levels—macro and micro—but also dividing qualitative methodology into two groups—(1) *formal*: systematic and rigorous data collection and analysis based on realist ontology and epistemology; and (2) *informal*: impressionistic procedures relying on descriptions of participants' overt behavior and statements based on postmodern constructionist ontology and epistemology. He conceives each dimension of cultural psychology theory and methodology on a continuum to form a typology of qualitative methods in cultural psychology. Both macro and micro cultural psychology can utilize formal and informal qualitative methodology resulting in the following classification system with four quadrants, which is briefly summarized below in Table 3.

Based on Bronfenbrenner's (1978) model, Ratner (2008b) suggests, ideally, micro level processes are nested within macro cultural psychology. Unfortunately, he observes micro cultural psychologists (e.g., many discursive psychologists) only focus on what participants think and say and neglect social and cultural origins that organize people's form and content of thought, choice, feeling and even subjectivity because of the assumption that individuals are free to construct their own psychological, interpersonal, and social lives. Just as qualitative methodology is diverse, narrative as well as other qualitative approaches, such as phenomenological and grounded theory, are also diverse, which is challenging to navigate, especially for those who are new to the field. Although Rather's (2008b) typology may be very restrictive in considering the integration of macro cultural psychology theory and formal qualitative methodology only acceptable, it provides one way to see how assumptions underlying theory/paradigm and methodology are intimately bound together.

Morrow (2005) suggests another framework to group and compare across three major paradigms in qualitative methodology based on the principle guiding the "quality" in qualitative research. Criteria such as internal validity, generalizability, reliability, and objectivity are used to judge quality in

TABLE 3 Ratner's typology of qualitative methods in cultural psychology

	Formal qualitative methodology	Informal qualitative methodology
Macro Cultural Psychology Theory Psychology is organized by macro cultural factors (e.g., social institutions, artifacts, and cultural concepts)	Systematically uses qualitative methods to elicit psychological expressions that (more often implicitly) contain cultural content derived from macro cultural factors; interpretation is also systematically derived from empirical data in a transparent manner (e.g., some critical hermeneutic and interpretive analysis)	Informally gathers fragmentary behavior and impressionistic scattered response, rather than systematically eliciting and analyzing a full range of interrelated behaviors, which results in ambiguous psychological and cultural content (e.g., many ethnographic studies)
Micro Cultural Psychology Theory Psychology is organized by individual and interpersonal relations	Employs qualitative methods rigorously to identify individual subject's construction of meanings and self on the basis of individualistic and interpersonal process; the mechanics of conversation is systematically documented but analyzed in a noncultural, abstract fashion rather than reflecting social meaning (i.e., does not interpret statements or relate them to cultural or psychological processes; resembles positivism's focus on overt behavior) (e.g., some discursive/discourse analysis)	Informal usage of qualitative methods to mainly depict individuals constructing personal meaning in a noncultural, abstract fashion (e.g., most discursive/discourse analysis)

quantitative research, but because they are not suitable for qualitative research, trustworthiness is utilized instead (Denzin & Lincoln, 2000; Patton, 2014). Morrow shows that the criteria of "trustworthiness" (also commonly referred to as validity by post-positivists) varies according to paradigm as indicated in Table 4.

TABLE 4 Morrow's paradigm-specific criteria of trustworthiness

Paradigm	Postpositivism	Interpretivism-Constructivism	Postmodern Critical-Ideological
Criteria of Trustworthiness (Validity)	Credibility Transferability Dependability Confirmability	Fairness Authenticities Ontological Educative Catalytic Tactical Meaning Verstehen Co-construction	Criteria from Interpretivism-Constructivism; Consequential Transgressive

While cross-cultural psychology research generally follows postpositivist assumptions, Ratner's (2008b) review of qualitative studies in cultural psychology seem to fall mainly under the interpretivism-constructivism and critical-ideological paradigms. Within this framework, he strongly advocates for distinguishing studies that incorporate macro cultural psychology theory and formal qualitative methodology employing rigorous, systematic data collection and analysis in contrast to those originating from the postmodern social constructionist view that valorizes individual, subjective construction of meaning uncritically based on nonsystematic, impressionistic data (Ratner, 2006). He identifies most discursive analyses fall under this category as indicated in Table 4.

Although the standard of trustworthiness is largely embedded in a specific paradigm, Morrow (2005) further points out that there are several broader criteria that "transcend" across paradigms, such as social validity, subjectivity and reflexivity, adequacy of data, and adequacy of interpretation. Due to the complexity of the subject, the nature of psychological research, in general, but cultural (religious) psychology research, in particular, require rigorous, systematic approach in both collecting and analyzing the data. However, similar to Ratner (2008a) and Belzen's (2001, 2010) observations, our review of recent journal articles on psychology and religion shows research that incorporates a (macro) cultural psychology perspective and formal qualitative methodology is indeed rare. Most investigations of religiosity utilize conventional theories and traditional research methods, which seldom provide substantial new insight, although the number of publications in reputable psychological journals is increasing.

Numerous scholars in the area of psychology and religion recommend that the rigorous, systematic (also described as meaning-structured, critical hermeneutic, interpretive) qualitative approach embraced by cultural psychology is vital for the future of the discipline (e.g., Browning, 2001; Belzen, 2001, 2010; Belzen & Hood, 2006; Straub & Weidemann, 2006). More specifically, narrative theory (e.g., Bruner, 1986; Howard, 1991; Polkinghorne, 1988; Sarbin, 1986) was instrumental not only in helping cultural psychology to shape a "meta-framework" for the field by adapting an interpretive human science approach (Hoshmand, 1996), but also in providing a way to integrate the relationship between culture (religion) and the individual, which has been a challenging problem for psychology, especially with rapid globalization (Hammack, 2008). For this reason, the remaining chapter will elaborate on narrative inquiry and systematic qualitative data collection and analysis, which can advance cultural psychology of religion.

4.4 *Narrative and Cultural Psychology of Religion*

Narratology is a term utilized to distinguish qualitative inquiry, which is derived from narrative theory and cultural psychology, from popular usage, referring to any written text or utterances (Hoshmand, 2005). Though the types of stories and methods used to study may vary, narrative researchers (e.g., Bruner, 1986; Howard, 1991; Polkinghorne, 1988; Sarbin, 1986) hold in common that the story is the fundamental unit that accounts for human experience and requires a temporal and causal coherence in meaning structure (Richardson, 2000). Based on Dewey's (1938) pragmatic philosophy, narrative inquiry understands experience as the fundamental ontological category characterized by interaction between "subject" and "object," self and world, and inner and outer elements. Because Dewey's ontology is transactional, it suggests the ideal inquiry is to produce a new relation or understanding between personal and social environment, not representation of a reality independent of the knower.

Clandinin and Connelly (2000) summarize "four turns toward narrative" in the following ways: (1) a change in the relationship between the researcher and the researched, (2) a move from the use of numbers toward the use of words as data, (3) a change from a focus on the general and universal toward the local and specific, and (4) a widening in acceptance of alternative epistemologies or ways of knowing. As a result, narrative inquiry arrives at a very different conception of knowledge than positivism (see Table 5).

TABLE 5 Comparison between positivism and narrative inquiry

	Positivism	Narrative inquiry
Knowledge	Seeks a description of a reality from outside a person's experience or independent of the knower (i.e., the only kinds of statements assuring certainty are descriptions of direct observation or that are deductively linked)	Seeks knowledge of human experience that remains within the lived experience
Temporality	Generally unable to capture the temporal quality, which is essential to understanding human experience; longitudinal study is an exception but is relatively rare due to time and cost intensiveness to conduct	Views events as happening over time; each event or thing has a past, present, and future
Action	Action is taken as directly evidential; an equation connecting action and meaning, connecting performance and cognitive level	An interpretive pathway between action and meaning is mapped out in terms of narrative histories
Context	While the influence of context is acknowledged, the purpose of the research design is to limit attention to that context; an experimental design is considered the ideal, in which all contextual influences can be controlled or at least accounted for	Multiple contexts (spatial, cultural, social, institutional, place, people) are always present; a relational form of inquiry describes the way people go about making sense of their experience within these contexts, contributing to ongoing sense-making

Therefore, narrative inquiry seeks a knowledge of human experience that does not merely describe but simultaneously adds meaning to experience (i.e., goals or intentions are embedded in stories of situated action), whereas positivism seeks a description of a reality that stands outside human experience (i.e., representation of a reality independent of the knower). Just as Valsner (2014) argues methodology cannot be reduced to method or be manualized,

Hoshmand (2005) suggests it is better to consider narratology as "methodological principles" rather than simple techniques. For this reason, instead of narrowing down a specific procedure or instruction, it is more beneficial to understand the narratological concepts that guide research processes. Qualitative approaches are not only diverse, but also flexible, as procedures can be combined coherently with the research design selected for the study. In the remaining sections, general practices on qualitative data collection and analysis will be combined with narratological principles to provide some guidance in conducting narrative research.

4.5 *The Study of Human Experience*

As the area of study should determine the inquiry methods, it is important to keep in mind that qualitative methods are overall designed to study human experience. In fact, Polkinghorne (2005) stresses that "the unit of analysis in qualitative research is experience, not individuals or groups" (p. 139). Given the object of investigation is the "life-world" as lived, he explains a primary purpose of qualitative research is to describe and clarify experience, which is much more challenging to achieve than what most people assume because human experience is not only complex and multilayered, but also not neatly ordered. For this reason, traditional research utilizing questionnaires or short-answers only glean information at the surface, which is inadequate to obtain the richness and depth of an experience. In order to capture the fullness of experience, a rigorous, systematic exploration is required. While "data" implies information is directly accessible, Polkinghorne suggests "accounts" more accurately conveys the interactive process required between participant and researcher in qualitative investigation.

Narrative inquirers (Clandinin & Connelly, 2000; Polkinghorne, 1988) expound that narrative is particularly well suited for studying human experiences involving: (1) temporality (i.e., individual choices shaped by past experience or describing human experience as it unfolds through time), (2) continuity (i.e., experiences growing out of other experiences), and (3) social dimension (i.e., exploring the stories people live and tell, which are the result of cultural or religious influences on a person's inner life and their unique personal history). Belzen (2001) explains that because religiosity is inseparable from cultural tradition, the cultural historical view of activity is instrumental in connecting to psychological phenomena, and narrative psychology provides a pathway to analyze the meaning that organizes specific activities in individual lives. Belzen (1999) elaborates that investigation involving a topic such as religious "conversion" experience will show a particular form and meaning in one culture and another form and meaning in a different culture. Thus, he stresses it is critical to study the human subject as embedded in the beliefs, values, and rules of a particular community rather than as an isolated individual.

Moreover, when a study involves adult "conscious" choices (e.g., deconversion or switching to another faith), a narrative approach is beneficial to gather the individual's life history and analyze the meaning (Belzen, 2001). For example, in the life stories of first-generation Korean American Christian women in their midlives, the participants' concept of spiritual maturity changed over time (Kim & Pak, 2013). Narrative analysis showed that each participant's image of God and spirituality in their early years of immigration to the U.S. reflected their previous collectivistic cultural upbringing, which maintained communal spirituality and practice. As these women acculturated to American culture over several decades, they gradually chose to leave Korean ethnic churches and transitioned to other mainstream churches. Reflecting on their decision to switch congregations, these women described their motivation to seek an American faith community that emphasized nurturing their individual growth more than serving others. These participants' narratives captured their changing inner desires and needs as they adopted the Western notions of "spiritual maturity."

Narrative approach, thus, not only allows investigators to study individual lives in context, but also explores the dynamic process of how individuals engage and internalize the collective narrative of their in-group as well as deviate from a dominant or "master narrative" of their cultural surroundings (Hammack, 2008; McAdams, 2006). Globally, as many countries are undergoing profound social changes and religious transformation, a narrative approach can be a valuable way to deeply examine how cultural shifts are configuring and reconfiguring the religious and spiritual landscapes in individuals' lives. Because various culturally available religious "life forms" are handed down through stories and practiced in the context of religious traditions or groups, narrative inquiry holds rich possibilities for cultural psychology of religion researchers to conduct in-depth analysis and capture the "religious horizon of understanding," or system of interpretation and conduct that gives meaning to people's lives (Belzen, 2010).

4.6 *Hermeneutic Interpretation*

Earlier narrative theorists tended to focus on the linguistic and structural elements. However, they have shifted more toward meaning and a functional model that stress the cultural aspect of narrative accounts and a form of validity based on pragmatic, dialectical, or hermeneutic epistemology rather than unrestricted meaning-making and interpretation suggested by "radical constructivism" (Hoshmand, 2005). Hoshmand appears to share a similar concern noted by Ratner (2006) in his discussion regarding those particularly originating from postmodern social constructionist views, such as most discursive and discourse analyses.

In contrast, grounded in hermeneutic traditions, the narrative understanding of human experience, involves a "hermeneutic circle" (Heidegger, 1962), or a part-to-whole process where one expands understanding about self, other, and the world through dialogical engagement (Gadamer, 1994). In this sense, the knowledge generated by a narrative approach depends on the background of shared understandings and meanings, which is always partial and contingent, but also makes it possible to contextually capture the meaning-making processes and developmental changes (Hammack, 2008; Hoshmand, 2005; Polkinghorne, 2000). As narrative understanding and interpretation is revised in the context of cultural background and changing knowledge, it requires the ongoing cultivation and development of critical reflexivity.

Specifically, Ratner (2008) advocates for what he calls "cultural hermeneutics" to explicate dialectically how the whole social system is contained in psychological phenomena. Although structural violence, injustice, and oppression should not be ignored, Hammack (2008) argues macrosocial analysis alone is not sufficient, as one must connect to the individual level in order to make sense of meaning psychologically. In other words, there is a dialectical relationship between social, cultural, and historical development and individual development (Meacham, 1999; Riegel,1976). Because identity inherently contains surrounding cultural and religious ideologies and takes on a narrative structure, life narratives uniquely allow investigators to access not only the macrosocial reflected in stories, but also how individuals make meaning of experience and develop a coherent self (Bluck & Habermas, 2000; Hammack, 2008; McAdams, 1993, 2001). Thus, a narrative approach integrates the relationship between culture and individual and permits deeper analysis by synthesizing theoretical and empirical advancements from multidisciplinary perspectives (e.g., developmental, cognitive, personality, social, cultural).

4.7 *Autobiographical Memory and Life Story*

According to Bruner (1990), narrative is connected to deep structures of human existence and is a primary embodiment of our understanding of self, experience, and the world. Because all reason-based, persuasive communication requires narrative, he argues we are narrative beings before we learn to use rational symbols. Lakoff and Johnson (1980) similarly indicate that starting early in life, people construct a coherent narrative in such a way that their story becomes a metaphorical understanding of life. Further extending the theory, Polkinghorne (1988) explains narrative emplotment appears to yield a form of understanding of human experience, both individual and collective, that is not directly amenable to other forms of exposition or analysis. The reason for this has to do with the way narratives articulate not just isolated acts but whole sequences of events or episodes, thereby placing particular events within a framing context or history and temporal experiences which give meaning through the unifying action of narration. This form of contextualizing has been recognized as crucial to any form of understanding, and narrative has emerged as an increasingly influential and integrating paradigm in psychology (Hammack, 2008; Hoshmand, 1996; McAdams, 1993).

According to McAdams (2001), life stories develop and change across one's life course. Autobiographical memories of lifetime periods and events (also referred to as "chapters") are organized in relatively large segments, such as early childhood, adolescence, college, midlife, and old age. They not only include general happenings, but also self-defining memories encompassing personal strivings and goals. He describes:

> Human life is storied, conceived in terms of settings, scenes, characters, plots, and themes. Stories are ideally suited to capture how a human actor, endowed with consciousness and motivated by intention, enacts desires and beliefs and strives for goals over time and in social context. (p. 117)

In the life story, the narrative process of sequencing events and autobiographical reasoning to make sense of the narrative account merge together. Singer (2004) explains: "The accumulating knowledge that emerges from reasoning about our narrative memories yields a life story schema that provides causal, temporal, and thematic coherence to an overall sense of identity" (p. 442).

As individuals internalize an evolving life story and integrate the reconstructed past and imagined future with unity and purpose, a narrative identity is formed. Here, it is important to note that life story and narrative identity is not an individual creation, but a jointly constructed process, reflecting the cultural, social, and family context that provide meaning, values, and norms (McAdams, 1993).

Researchers (Bluck & Habermas, 2000; Nelson & Fivush, 2004; Wang & Brockmeier, 2002) show autobiographical remembering is a cultural practice. Just as cultural knowledge, symbols, and concepts are psychically organized as young children learn language, hear stories, develop schemes, and assimilate social conventions, individuals acquire a catalogue of "plots," including religious prescriptions, to interpret and make sense of their lives. Pak's (2006) narrative analysis of second-generation, Korean American, young women's life stories, for example, demonstrates how everyday "activities" are psychically internalized into roles and are configured to give life purpose and meaning. Although her participants externally appeared acculturated or "Americanized" at the behavioral level, their idea of "success" was shaped by traditional cultural notions of collective family security (e.g., financially able to provide for their aging parents and younger siblings) at the core values level. Interestingly, this definition of success was influenced by their earliest memories of stories they had heard growing up about their parents' initial struggles to survive in the U.S. as immigrants. Thus, their parents' experiences of marginal status and poverty set the tone for their motivation to "succeed" in the next generation.

An interesting discovery in Pak's (2006) study was that the interviewees' did not realize they had internalized their parents' insecurities despite organizing their life purpose and goals to find "security" for their family. Though the Confucian ideological practice of we-consciousness or collective family-oriented security is a common cultural practice among Korean families, these participants did not have explicit knowledge of what they embodied throughout their whole lives. This illustrates how cultural phenomena are multiplexed and deeply rooted in everyday practices, needs, and emotions, and people often cannot articulate at a verbal or cognitive level why they do what they do. According to Bourdieu (1980/1990), all psychological characteristics are personally embodied and organized to structure people's actions, which he calls *habitus*. Located deep in the body, people only have limited access to reflect. However, this very structure is where an individual and social, cultural, and religious institutions intersect (also see Steinmetz, 2014). Consequently, researchers are only able to tell half of the story without analyzing activity and meaning.

Because meanings behind cultural practices are not always available to participants, narrative research requires adeptness in not only gathering information both on and below the surface, but also connecting experience to deeper meaning structure. It may be appealing to simply collect and present personal stories with no analysis, but identifying the deep meaning structure actually helps the investigator unravel participants' accounts of experiences and comprehend many loose surface descriptions. Hoshmand (2005) argues, "the usefulness of narratives as data depends critically on the conceptual perspective in which narrative inquiry is framed and in the use of a narratological methodology that is made transparent to the reader" (p. 183). The life story interview provides a good overarching structure organized around large segments of time, while allowing flexibility to explore general and personal events and meanings within each time frame. It offers a general roadmap for the investigator to systematically collect participants' experiences sequentially; on the other hand, it also gives some space to roam and explore various pockets that are relevant for investigation with deeper reflection. The participant's account of experience collected at each stage can be triangulated with other experiences, examining consistencies and contradictions as well as how various themes from the early period evolve as life stages progress. Thus, in order to gather rich descriptions and accounts of life experiences, the interview needs to be viewed as an organic unfolding process like peeling an onion rather than a simple list of questions that can be manualized. Unlike structured interview, in semi-structured, in-depth interviews, the researcher develops a flexible interview protocol or guiding questions, but data collection still takes on a relational focus and allows exploration of participant thoughts, feelings, and beliefs about a particular topic by delving deeply into personal experiences (see Josselson, 2013; Kvale, 1996).

4.8 *Further Considerations in Data Collection and Analysis Process*

Although different qualitative data analysis techniques have generally received attention, the value of systematic data collection in qualitative research is not understood as well. However, without a rigorous, thoughtful data gathering process, it is not possible to obtain a meaningful narrative account of the participant's experience, which requires closer examination. Even though it is common practice to utilize self-reports in psychology, Polkinghorne (2005) notes important limitations of such accounts, which largely depends on the interviewee's ability to reflect and communicate their own experience. He explains:

> Although self-report evidence is necessary and valuable for inquiry about human experience, it is not to be misconstrued as mirrored reflections of experience. People do not have complete access to their experiences. The capacity to be aware of or to recollect one's experiences is intrinsically limited. People do not have a clear window into their inner life. (p. 139)

Despite these limitations, narrative theorists, such as Ricoeur (1977), indicate that language is the primary mechanism to gain access to complex human experiences, even if it is only partial. Because the goal of qualitative research is to enrich the understanding of an experience, not to collect the most data, a set of principles guide the data gathering process, such as purposeful or theoretical sampling of participants to ensure information rich cases rather than the random selection method commonly used in quantitative studies (Patton, 2014; Polkinghorne, 2005). To deepen the understanding of the experience investigated, a small number of participants, for example, with maximum variation could be employed to compare and contrast different perspectives which can serve as a kind of triangulation on the experience.

Interview is the most common form of data collection used in qualitative research, but triangulating other sources of data, such as observations and documents, are also important. In his study of the Christian serpent handling tradition, it was most impressive that Hood (2008) observed the community, including their worship services, for over five years before conducting his first interview (personal communication, June, 2014). This example demonstrates how critical observation is, especially when one is investigating an unfamiliar subject or faith community. However, because most doctoral students do not have five years to observe the phenomena under study, students could be encouraged to identify areas of investigation they are personally familiar with or have observed for many years whenever possible. The researcher's "bias" is important to be aware of and should be addressed by using triangulation methods, such as keeping memos (a journal of researcher's observations and activities) throughout the research process and a research team for accountability. However, maintaining "objective" distance is more problematic not only in terms of resulting in surface level analysis, but also, more importantly, the researcher's unarticulated implicit bias or assumptions. For other triangulation methods (e.g., data, investigator, theory, methodological) that could be combined to add rigor and gain a comprehensive understanding of a phenomena under study, a general handbook on qualitative research is recommended (e.g., Denzin & Lincoln, 2000; Patton, 2014).

A common misunderstanding related to gathering "data" is treating it as though participants' experiential account is just on the surface ready for researchers to simply collect them; the interview process, however, actually requires much more time and effort to access information and meaning behind events, which is not unlike the therapeutic situation (McClelland, 2017; Polkinghorne, 2005). While psychotherapy and qualitative research both involve skill such as building rapport and active listening to direct the flow of the conversation and reflect on the experience, what sets these two apart is the purpose of study should guide the researcher in gathering information from the participant (Kvale, 1996; Polkinghorne, 2005). The semi-structured interview format is often utilized to guide the process in qualitative research; however, this cannot be reduced to a set of techniques or instructions because the researcher needs to be fully present, exercise judgment to skillfully adjust questions, and help explore as the interview progresses.

In the qualitative research, the investigator stays open throughout the process by iteratively weaving data collection and analysis together until a rich description or a theory of the phenomena under study emerges (Denzin & Lincoln, 2000; Patton, 2014; Polkinghorne, 2005).

Because interviewing a participant only once for an hour is seldom adequate to obtain a full account of the experience and reflect on the meaning, an iterative process is applied not only across participants or multiple cases, but also within a case by carrying out a sequence of three interviews with each participant (Polkinghorne, 2005; Seidman, 1991). The first interview is mainly used to get acquainted, build rapport, introduce the study topic, and lay out the framing questions. As the participant has time to think about the experience in between the meetings, the second interview generally allows the researcher to explore and help focus on the account more deeply. Finally, the third interview provides an opportunity to not only ask follow-up questions and clarifications, but also reflect on the whole experience and process the meaning.

Through an in-depth interview, Polkinghorne (2005) states "a loosely linked collection of descriptions, explanations, and stories" are used to produce a *narrative account* with the following characteristics: (1) a storied form containing a beginning-middle-end structure; and (2) descriptions of events or happenings that are tied together to present a plot that contributes to the story's thematic meaning involving *a narrative mode of understanding* (p. 142). While paradigmatic mode employs categorization and seeks to explain and predict the underlying relationships between sets of observable factors, narrative mode focuses on capturing the shifting contours of lived experience and the meaning that is assigned to experiences through stories (Polkinghorne, 1988). Narrative strives to capture people's own explanations about what they want and how they go about achieving it, and it seeks to explain the storied meaning people make of these relationships. Polkinghorne stresses the holistic, interpretive narrative analysis with a part-to-whole configuration should produce a storied account, which distinguishes it from other types of analysis.

Hoshmand (2005) indicates narrative data based on a narrative mode of understanding could be combined with a paradigmatic mode in the theorizing stage (i.e., inductive-thematic-theory-generating) to produce varying degrees of "story-likeness" in the final reporting. In this way, she suggests narratological methodology can be used with other qualitative approaches (e.g., grounded theory, thematic analysis, phenomenological), but the recounting of life experience is a general requirement for an intelligible story. One way to revise and explore new theory through connecting the individual with culture includes creatively combining narrative and case study methods (see Pak, 2006). For example, first, each participant can be treated as a distinct individual case study using a narrative mode of understanding; a sequence of three in-depth life story interviews and narrative analyses can then be carried out to explore within each case as deeply as possible to produce a storied account of the individual's experience. Next, more cases are added until saturation is reached or additional new data no longer expands or challenges the finding. After this component of the investigation is complete, a paradigmatic mode of analysis could be applied to multiple cases in order to compare across emerging themes and generate a theory. In this way, just as qualitative and quantitative research could be combined in a mixed-method approach, inductive and deductive analysis could be incorporated to complement and strengthen an empirical investigation.

As Lamiell (2019) suggested, rigorous analyses of single cases could be used to critically examine and generate new theory. One project involving a single case study illustrates this point (Schuberg & Pak, in preparation). Existing theory and empirical investigation on spiritual doubt, especially in the context of a particular religion, is currently very limited. Analyzing a case of a participant's life story growing up in the Catholic faith tradition revealed how spiritual doubt and conflicts are so deeply intertwined throughout one's life that it is impractical to separate and lose the rich meaning behind spiritual struggles. Moreover, religious identification reflected early attachments not only to significant relationships, but also to specific places and historical time (e.g., the post-WWII Europe, the 60's in the West Coast of the U.S., etc.). The complexity of topics, such as spiritual doubt, shows the need for robust engagement with a participant in a context that allows investigators to gain a deeper understanding of particular phenomena in theory development rather than "objective" distancing of data (Alvesson & Karreman, 2007).

Increasingly, investigators are called to critically examine existing psychological theories and explore the cultural, religious, and psychological structures and processes in a more in-depth way (e.g., Stainton Rogers & Willig, 2017; Hood & Williamson, 2008; Belzen, 1999). Although the individual person has been long recognized as the unit of analysis in psychology, the rise of statistical methods has led to the dominance of nomothetic research, which some scholars have argued resulted in the current disciplinary crisis (Belzen & Hood, 2006; Hammack, 2008; Valsner, 2014). Because narrative inquiry takes into account the participant's unique life experience in a rich context, it is particularly suited to help understand the individual case more in-depth in ways that are normally not possible in traditional research. As greater interdisciplinary integration and methodological innovations are necessary to keep the field viable, narrative inquiry has much to offer future directions in cultural psychology of religion.

5 Conclusion: Towards Theoretical and Methodological Diversity in American Psychology of Religion

As modern psychology emerged in primarily Western industrialized countries over the last hundred years and is indigenous to the North American and European context, theoretical and methodological innovation is critical now more than ever in the global era (Arnett, 2008; Dueck, 2007; Lawson et al., 2007). A critical problem in American psychology is recognizing ethnocentricity and its value-laden shortcomings, and psychology of religion is no exception.

According to Hood (2000), the psychology of religion was founded in the U.S., and shaped the field, but "the history of the psychology of religion in America and the definition of the discipline remain problematic" because it has been less of a disciplinary movement and more of an interest sustained by a few prominent investigators (p. 531). Even in recent times, he argues *Journal for the Scientific Study of Religion* (JSSR), for example, is an outlet for publication for a few psychologists interested in researching religion due to a lack of acceptance in mainstream psychological journals; consequently, in order to escape marginal status, there has been a greater pressure for "a methodological rigor that demands only reductive explanations" (p. 538) among religionists.

Our review of published studies in major journals on psychology and religion not only confirms Hood's (2000) comments, but also shows the particular cultural context in which individuals' religious/spiritual experiences are deeply intertwined is rarely acknowledged or incorporated in research, even as investigators in this area may focus on "religion" or "spirituality." Hence, the observation Belzen (2010) made more than a decade ago sadly still holds true—that even though religion is one of the most complex, culturally constituted phenomena expressed psychically, little progress has been made in terms of researchers taking the recommendation seriously that "no single form of religious psychic functioning can be properly understood without taking cultural factors into account" and psychology of religion must move toward "cultural inclusiveness in its theories and methods" (p. 17).

5.1 *Qualitative Inquiry and Psychology*

In the late nineteenth and early twentieth centuries, psychologists adopted the single philosophy of science viewing natural science as the only proper "scientific" psychology and blindly upheld universality, objectivity, and stability of behavior (Cole, 1996; Leahey, 2000; Polkinghorne, 1983; Stainton Rogers & Willig, 2017). Although qualitative research has been part of modern psychology from the beginning, it was obscured as quantitative research came to dominate the field. Psychology became preoccupied with measurement and statistics despite warnings of misuse, such as drawing wrong generalizations from group to individuals (Danziger, 1990; Lamiell, 1981, 2019; Leary, 2014; Stainton Rogers & Willig, 2017; Wertz, 2014).

For more than a century, Continental philosophers have fought to establish human sciences in the discipline and proposed methodological reform appropriate to study human experience and action that is embodied, historical, and integral (Cole, 1996; Polkinghorne, 1988). However, psychologists persisted in relying exclusively on natural science methods and marginalizing qualitative inquiry, which has had devastating consequences for the discipline as a whole (Polkinghorne, 1983; Wertz, 2011). Although deductive reasoning has been valued for its precision due to a strong commitment to positivist epistemology and methodology, it is more problematic in most psychological investigations involving complex, interrelated concepts that require deeper understanding of human experience and meaning, such as those found in cultural psychology and religion (Belzen & Hood, 2006; Pak, 2017; Polkinghorne, 1983). Unlike the physical and biological realm, the appropriateness of seeking reductionistic, universal knowledge in psychology has been seriously challenged because higher mental processes, such as beliefs, values, and choices, are bound by their historical and cultural context (Gergen, 1973; Polkinghorne, 1983; Taylor, 1992).

Polkinghorne (1983) argues human knowledge is always conditional and context-bound in that all knowledge is constructed within one's conceptual, linguistic, and cultural system. Thus, regardless of quantitative or qualitative research, "pure data" or facts do not exist apart from interpretation, theory, or other elements of preunderstanding (e.g., social, political, research community); for this reason, Alvesson and Skoldberg (2017) emphasize that the most valuable aspects of research are interpretive, reflexive, and active engagement with participants to gain a deeper understanding of particular phenomena rather than objective distancing. Thus, "good science" is not the accumulation of facts but requires openness, creativity, humility, and patience in interacting with data beyond the surface level in order to critically break down existing theory, assumptions, and bias for new theory to emerge (Alvesson & Skoldberg, 2017; Davis, 2009; Leary, 2014).

5.2 *Psychology of Religion and Culture*

Viewing religion as overlapping with moral ethical background beliefs in modern social sciences, Browning (2001) suggests the field of religion and psychological studies can best achieve its full potential through "critical hermeneutics" to engage in rigorous dialogue and understanding to address contemporary social problems. Ratner (2008) similarly advocates for what he calls "cultural hermeneutics" to explicate dialectically how the whole social system is contained in psychological phenomena. Hammack (2008), on the other hand, emphasizes macrosocial analysis alone is not sufficient, as it must connect to the individual level in order to make sense of meaning psychologically. Similar to Belzen and Hood (2006), these authors all strongly argue that in order to produce a real paradigm shift in the field, it is crucial to orient toward the pragmatic, dialectical, hermeneutic epistemology or qualitative interpretive tradition and pay more attention to the particularities of religion and culture in the real-world context. Though they may vary slightly in what they emphasize, they all agree, unlike the lower level structure (e.g., behaviorism, computational cognitive psychology, etc.), theories at the higher level increasingly require integration of human consciousness, culture, and history and a multilevel interdisciplinary paradigm in order to adequately capture and interpret the activities and experiences studied; human lives must be situated and understood in their specific cultural, historical, and religious setting. Thus, methodological pluralism has been emphasized to develop an integrative paradigm for the study of the psychology of religion and spirituality.

According to Wulff (2003), the current state of psychology of religion research is in "crisis" and needs to "start over" as the field has lost theoretical depth and methodological breadth. In spite of globalization, religion is intimately bound with cultural tradition, especially in the non-Western world, and a different kind of research is required than what is commonly practiced. Building culturally robust and intelligible theories capable of responding more effectively and sensitively to complex problems faced by a rapidly changing world calls for openness in theoretical innovation and methodological diversity (Belzen & Hood, 2006; Valsner, 2014). Interestingly, prior to the dominance of hypothetico-deductivism, science was originally conceptualized much more broadly as a systematic, rigorous activity to produce trustworthy knowledge, and qualitative methodology was accepted as equally valid and empirical (Stainton Rogers & Willig, 2017). Thus, the call for a "new" start in psychology of religion may be a return to the beginning, before psychology adopted natural science as the only proper "scientific" psychology (Wertz, 2011), that also moves forward by extending issues faced by the global community and current practices in international research.

5.3 *Cultural Psychology and Narrative Inquiry*

For the last two decades, cultural psychologists have raised the problem in over utilizing methods developed out of the natural sciences to compare peoples across cultures and search for invariable psychic structures (e.g., Belzen, 2010; Cole, 1996; Ratner, 2008). Deeply rooted in cultural-historical, dialectical, and hermeneutic philosophy, cultural psychology as an interpretive discipline stresses the importance of context for meaning (Belzen, 2001; Rater, 2008a; Shweder, 1991; Straub & Weidemann, 2006). Cultural psychologists conceive culture psychologically as a meaning-structed "hermeneutic concept" and view human behavior to be meaningful only when interpreted in its social-cultural context, taking into an account environment, history, culture, and complexity of real-life activity (Straub & Weidemann, 2006). Based on Vygotsky's (1978) cultural-historical theory, cultural psychology emphasizes that psychological phenomena, particularly higher mental functions, are subjective manifestations of cultural activity and products of historical development. Unlike cross-cultural psychology, cultural psychology does not treat culture as an independent variable but as an interpretive concept; rather than focusing on measuring *behavior* (stimulus-response), it conceives of culture on a different level by studying *action* (situated) (Rater, 2008a). It is important to note that action not only situates the context in a holistic sense, but also contains the notion of goals, purpose, and intention, which requires an organizing principle that is faithful to the complexities observed when people engage in intentional performances to realize their often unarticulated goals.

The meaning-structures of culture and culturally mediated actions on cognitions, emotions, and motivations not only require psychology to reassess its object, but also its methodology (Belzen, 2001; Ratner, 2008b; Straub & Weidemann, 2006). Grounded in hermeneutic traditions, the narrative understanding of human experience involves a part-to-whole process where one expands understanding of self, other, and the world through dialogical engagement (Gadamer, 1994; Heidegger, 1962). In this sense, the knowledge generated by narrative approach depends on the background of shared understandings and meanings, which is always partial and contingent, but also makes it possible to capture the meaning-making processes and developmental changes contextually (Hammack, 2008; Hoshmand, 2005; Polkinghorne,

2000). Historically, narrative theorists tended to focus on the linguistic and structural elements, but this has shifted more to the meaning and functional model, which stresses the cultural aspect of narrative accounts and a form of validity based on pragmatic, dialectical, or hermeneutic epistemology rather than unrestricted meaning-making and interpretation as suggested by "radical constructivism" (Hoshmand, 2005; Ratner, 2006).

Adapting an interpretive human science approach, narrative theory (e.g., Bruner, 1986; Howard, 1991; Polkinghorne, 1988; Sarbin, 1986) offers a "meta-framework" for the field to integrate advancements from diverse areas such as developmental, cognitive, personality, social, and cultural psychology (Hammack, 2008; Hoshmand, 1996; McAdams, 2001). Because identity inherently contains one's cultural and religious ideological surroundings and takes on a narrative structure, life narratives uniquely allow investigators to access not only the macrosocial reflected in the stories, but also how individuals make meaning of experiences and develop a coherent self (Hammack, 2008; McAdams, 1993, 2001). As individuals internalize an evolving life story and integrate the reconstructed past and imagined future with unity and purpose, identity develops; however, it is important to note that life story and narrative identity are not individual achievements but rather jointly constructed processes reflecting family, social, and cultural practices, which provide meaning, values, and norms (Bluck & Habermas, 2000; McAdams, 1993; Nelson & Fivush, 2004; Pak, 2006; Wang & Brockmeier, 2002). Thus, narrative approach allows integration of the dynamic relationship between culture (religion) and the individual as well as rich understanding of human experience and development synthesizing multidisciplinary perspectives.

Narrative inquiry is particularly well suited for studying human experiences involving temporality, continuity, and social dimension (Clandinin & Connelly, 2000; Polkinghorne, 1988). Narrative appears to yield a form of understanding of human experience, both individual and collective, that is not directly amenable to other forms of exposition or analysis. The reason for this has to do with the way narratives articulate not just isolated acts but whole sequences of events or episodes, thereby placing particular events within a framing context or history and temporal experiences which give meaning through the unifying action of narration (Polkinghorne, 1988). This form of contextualizing has been recognized as crucial to any form of understanding, and narrative has emerged as an increasingly influential and integrating paradigm in psychology (Hammack, 2008; Hoshmand, 1996; McAdams, 1993).

5.4 *Future Directions*

The nature of psychological research in general, but cultural (religious) psychology research in particular due to complexity of subject, requires rigorous, systematic approach. However, similar to Ratner (2008a) and Belzen's (2001, 2010) observations, our review of recent journal articles on psychology and religion shows this type of research incorporating a (macro) cultural psychology perspective and formal qualitative methodology is indeed rare. As much as "formal" or rigorous and systematic investigation in qualitative research is advocated for, it is important to keep in mind that quality or "validity" in qualitative inquiry is paradigm bound (Morrow, 2005). If publishers, journal editors, and readers continue to adopt a "single science" view and only utilize a postpositivist paradigm to judge qualitative articles, two unfortunate results will occur. First, the mixed-method approach will be automatically assumed as "rigorous" and all investigators will be expected to include both qualitative and quantitative data collection and analysis. As our review showed, most mixed-method studies in psychology of religion rarely treated qualitative inquiry as a complementary or "equal partner" in the investigation and often employed some open-ended questions tagged on at the end of a quantitative survey (see Streib & Hood, 2015 for an excellent example of rigorous triangulation of mixed-methods in theory development). Second, qualitative studies based on other paradigms, such as interpretivism-constructivism and critical-ideological, will be rejected as methodologically inadequate, and a gross underrepresentation of qualitative research in psychology of religion will persist. As we have seen, most investigations on religiosity in the U.S. utilized conventional theories and traditional research methods, which seldom provided substantial, new insight, although the number of publications in reputable psychological journals is increasing. Even though Europe, Australia, and Canada are more open and appreciative of contributions offered by qualitative research from diverse paradigms, it is challenging for researchers to network and submit articles to international journals they are less familiar with. More support for international research and scholarship is needed in the future to encourage more robust exchanges of ideas and theories that build from diverse perspectives and contexts in psychology of religion.

The purpose of qualitative inquiry is understanding not only diverse human experiences in cultural contexts, but also new or hard-to-define phenomena related to meaning, purpose, intentionality, and spirituality and revealing their deep structure (Polkinghorne, 1983; Denzin & Lincoln, 2000; Davis, 2009; Josselson, 2014; Stainton Rogers & Willig, 2017; Pak, 2017; Thin, 2018). Increasingly, investigators are called to critically examine existing psychological theories and explore the cultural, religious, and psychological structures and processes in more in-depth way. Although the individual person has been long recognized as the unit of analysis in psychology, the rise of statistical methods has led to the dominance of nomothetic research which some scholars have argued resulted in the current disciplinary crisis (Belzen & Hood, 2006; Hammack, 2008; Valsiner, 2014).

Because narrative inquiry takes into account the participant's unique life experience in rich context, it is particularly suited to help understand the individual case more in-depth in ways it is normally not possible in traditional research. As religiosity is inseparable from cultural tradition, the cultural historical view of activity is instrumental in connecting to psychological phenomena, and narrative psychology provides a way to analyze the meaning that organizes specific activities in individual lives. Greater interdisciplinary integration and methodological innovations are necessary to keep the field viable, and narrative inquiry has much to offer future directions in cultural psychology of religion with new integrative understanding, theory building, and social change.

Acknowledgements

Many thanks to Ralph W. Hood, Jr. for the encouragement to write this monograph and his most generous and unwavering support, without which it could not have come to fruition. I am indebted to Donald Polkinghorne who nurtured the value of qualitative inquiry and narrative analysis as my chair more than two decades ago, and his influence is apparent throughout this monograph. I would like to also thank my doctoral student Miriam S. Kang, at Fuller Graduate School of Psychology, for her contribution, without which the "Review of Qualitative Research in Psychology of Religion" section 3 could not have been written. In a year's time, she worked tirelessly to not only learn qualitative research paradigms and diverse approaches, but also code over one-hundred journal articles. I am truly grateful for her assistance and unflagging enthusiasm. I also appreciate my daughter Morgan who contributed through proofreading and many other forms of support, a testimony to her patience and kindness.

References

Allport, G. W. (1942). The use of personal documents in psychological science. Prepared for the Committee on the Appraisal of Research. Bulletin #49, New York, NY: Social Science Council.

Allwood, C. M., & Berry, J. W. (2006). Origins and development of indigenous psychologies: An international analysis. *International Journal of Psychology*, 41, 243–268.

Alvesson, M., & Karreman, D. (2007). Constructing mystery: Empirical matters in theory development. *Academy of Management Review*, 32(4), 1265–1281.

Alvesson, M., & Sköldberg, K. (2017). *Reflexive Methodology*. London: Sage.

American Psychological Association. (2002). Guidelines on multicultural education, training, research, practice and organizational change for psychologists. Washington, DC: American Psychological Association.

American Psychological Association. (2009). *Guidelines and principles for accreditation of programs in professional psychology*. Washington, DC: American Psychological Association.

Arnett, J. J. (2008). The neglected 95%: Why American psychology needs to become less American. *American Psychologist*, 63(7), 602–614.

Aten, J. D., & Hernandez, B. C. (2005). A 25-year review of qualitative research published in spirituality and psychologically oriented journals. *Journal of Psychology and Christianity*, 24, 266–277.

Azari, N. P., & Birnbacher, D. (2004). The role of cognition and feeling in religious experience. *Zygon: Journal of Religion and Science*, 39(4), 901–917.

Baker, D. (2008). *Korean spirituality*. Honolulu: University of Hawaii Press.

Bannister, R. (1987). *Sociology and scientism: The American quest for objectivity, 1880–1940*. Chapel Hill: University of North Carolina Press.

Belzen, J. A. (1999). Religion as embodiment: Cultural-psychological concepts and methods in the study of conversion among "bevindelijken". *Journal for the Scientific Study of religion*, 38(2), 236–253.

Belzen, J. (2001). The future is in the return: Back to cultural psychology of religion. In D. Jonte-Pace & W. B. Parsons (Eds.), *Religion and psychology: Mapping the terrain*, (pp. 43–56). New York: Routledge.

Belzen, J. A. (2010). *Towards cultural psychology of religion: Principles, approaches, applications*. New York: Springer.

Belzen, J. A., & Hood, R. W. Jr. (2006). Methodological issues in the psychology of religion: Toward another paradigm? *The Journal of Psychology*, 140, 5–28.

Berry, A., Francis, L. J., Rolph, J., & Rolph, P. (2012). Ministry and Stress: Listening to Anglican Clergy in Wales. *Pastoral Psychology*, 61(2), 165–178.

Berry, J. W., Poortinga, Y. H., & Pandey, J. (Eds.) (1997). *Handbook of cross-cultural psychology*. Boston: Allyn & Bacon.

Bluck, S., & Habermas, S. (2000). Getting a life: The emergence of the life story in adolescence. *Psychological Bulletin*, 126(5), 748–769. doi: 10.1037/0033-2909.126.5.748.

Brahinsky, J. (2018). How Western agency-anxieties mold affect theory, and how Pentecostalism and neuroscience teach us to think differently. *Anthropological Theory*, 18(4), 478–501.

Breen, G. M. (2008). Interpersonal, Intragroup Conflict between Southern Baptist Pastors: A Qualitative Inquiry Examining Contributing Factors. *Pastoral Psychology*, 56(3), 249–268.

Bronfenbrenner, U. (1979). *The ecology of human development*. Cambridge: Harvard University Press.

Browning, D. (2001). The past and possible future of religion and psychological studies. In W. B. Parsons, D. E., & Jonte-Pace (Eds.), *Religion and psychology: Mapping the Terrain* (pp., 165–180). New York: Routledge.

Bruner, J. S. (1986). *Actual minds, possible worlds*. Cambridge, MA: Harvard University Press.

Bruner, J. S. (1990). *Acts of meaning*. Cambridge, MA: Harvard University Press.

Charmaz, K. (2000). Grounded theory: Objectivist and constructivist methods. In N. K. Denzin & Y. S. Lincoln (Eds.), *Handbook of qualitative research* (2nd ed., pp. 509–535). Thousand Oaks, CA: Sage.

Charmaz K. (2006). Constructing grounded theory: a practical guide through qualitative analysis. Thousand Oaks, CA: Sage.

Chibber, V. (2013). *Postcolonial theory and the specter of capital*. London: Verso.

Clore, G. L. (2011). Psychology and rationality of emotion. *Modern Theology*, 27(2), 325–338.

Cole, M. (1996). *Cultural psychology: A once and future discipline*. Cambridge, Mass: Harvard University Press.

Comas-Diaz, L., & Rivers, E. T. (2020). (Eds.) *Liberation psychology: Theory, method, practice, and social justice*. Washington, DC: American Psychological Association.

Crenshaw, M. R. (2015). Attitudes of African American Clergy Regarding the Postvention Needs of African American Suicide Survivors. *Pastoral Psychology*, 64(2), 169–183.

Creswell, J. W., & Plano Clark, V. L. (2nd ed.). (2010). *Designing and conducting mixed methods research*. Thousand Oaks, CA: Sage.

Cumming, G., Fidler, F., Leonard, M., Kalinowski, P., Christiansen, A., Kleinig, A., Lo, J., McMenamin, N., & Wilson, S. (2007). Statistical reform in psychology: Is anything changing? *Psychological Science*, 18(3), 230–232.

d'Aquili, E. G., & Newberg, A. B. (1999). The neuropsychological basis of religions, or why god won't go away. *Zygon*, 33(2), 187–201.

Dahl, C. M., Jensen, M. L., & McCampbell, J. L. (2010). A butterfly effect: The impact of marriage and family therapy training on students' spouses. *Journal of Psychology and Theology*, 38(1), 3–14.

Damasio, A. (1999). *The feeling of what happens.* San Diego and New York: Harcourt.

Danziger, K. (1983). Origins and basic principles of Wundt's Völkerpsychologie. *British Journal of Social Psychology*, 22, 303–313.

Danziger, K. (1990) *Constructing the subject: Historical origins of psychological research.* Cambridge: Cambridge University Press.

Davis, E. B., Cuthbert, A. D., Hays, L. W., Aten, J. d., Van Tongerren, D. R., Hook, J. N ... Boan, D. (2016). Using qualitative and mixed methods to study relational spirituality. *Psychology of Religion and Spirituality*, 8, 92–98.

Davis, J. (2009). Complementary research methods in humanistic and transpersonal psychology: A case for methodological pluralism. *The Humanistic Psychologist*, 37, 4–23.

Denzin, N. K., & Lincoln, Y. S. (Eds.). (2000). *Handbook of qualitative research.* Thousand Oaks, CA: Sage.

Devereux, G. (1967). *From anxiety to method in the behavioral sciences.* Hague, Paris: Mouton & Co.

Dilthey, W. (1900/1979). The rise of hermeneutics. Translated by Thomas Hall. In P. Connerton (Ed.), *Critical Sociology* (pp. 104–116). N.Y.: Penguin Books.

Dueck, A. (1995). *Between Jerusalem and Athens: Ethical perspectives on culture, religion, and psychotherapy.* Grand Rapids: Baker Books.

Dueck, A. (2007). Constantine, Babel, and Yankee doodling: Whose indigeneity? Whose psychology? *Pastoral Psychology*, 56, 66–72.

Dueck, A., & Reimer, K. (2009). *A peaceable psychology.* Grand Rapids, MI: Brazos Press.

Emmons, R. A. & Paloutzian, R. F. (2003). The psychology of religion. *Annual Review of Psychology*, 54, 377–402. https://doi-org.fuller.idm.oclc.org/10.1146/annurev.psych.54.101601.145024.

Enriquez, V. G. (1992). *From colonial to liberation psychology: The Philippine experience.* Quezon City, The Philippines: University of the Philippines Press.

Fanon, F. (1967). *Black skins, white masks.* New York, NY: Grove Press.

Filstead, W. J. (1979). Qualitative methods: A needed perspective in evaluation research. In T. D. Cook & C. S. Reichardt (Eds.), *Qualitative and quantitative methods in evaluation research* (pp. 33–48). Beverly Hills, CA: Sage.

Flyvbjerg, B. (2006). Five misunderstandings about case-study research. *Qualitative Inquiry*, 12(2), 219–245. doi:10.1177/1077800405284363.

Freeman, M. (2016). Narrative psychology as science and as art. In J. Valsiner, G. Mariscico, N. Chaudhary, T. Sato, & V. Dazzani (Eds)., *Psychology as the science of human being: The Yokohama manifesto* (pp. 349–364). Springer.

Gadamer, H. G. (1994). *Truth and method* (J. Weinsheimer & D. G. Marshall, Trans.). (2nd ed.). New York: Seabury Press.

Geertz, C. (1973). Thick description: Toward an interpretive theory of culture. In C. Geertz, *The interpretation of cultures* (pp. 3–30). New York: Basic Books.

Gergen, K. J. (1973). Social psychology as history. *Journal of Personality and Social Psychology*, 26(2), 309–320.

Gergen, K. J. (2014). Pursuing excellence in qualitative inquiry. *Qualitative Psychology*, 1(1), 49–60.

Gergen, K. J., Gulerce, A., Lock, A., & Misra, G. (1996). Psychological science in cultural context. *American Psychologist*, 51(5), 496–503.

Gergen, K. J., Josselson, R., & Freeman, M. (2015). The promises of qualitative inquiry. *American Psychologist*, 70, 1–9.

Gilligan, C. (1982). *In a Different Voice*. Cambridge, MA: Harvard University Press.

Giorgi, A. (2009). *The descriptive phenomenological method in psychology: A modified Husserlian approach*. Pittsburgh, PA: Duquesne University Press.

Glaser, B. G., & Strauss, A. L. (1967). *The discovery of grounded theory: Strategies for qualitative research*. New York: Aldine.

Goertz, G., & Mahoney, J. (2012). *A tale of two cultures: Qualitative and quantitative research in the social sciences*. Princeton: Princeton University Press.

Gorsuch, R. L. (1984). Measurement: The boon and bane of investigating religion. *American Psychologist*, 39, 228–36.

Grayson, J. H. (2006). A quarter-millennium of Christianity in Korea. In R. E. Buswell, Jr. & T. S. Lee (Eds.), *Christianity in Korea* (pp. 7–25). Honolulu, University of Hawaii Press.

Gross, J. J. (2001). Emotion regulation in adulthood: Timing is everything. *Current Directions in Psychological Science*, 10, 214–19.

Hammack, P. (2008). Narrative and cultural psychology of identity. *Personality and Social Psychology Review*, 12, 222–247.

Hansen, J. T. (2004). Thoughts on knowing: Epistemic implications of counseling practice. *Journal of Counseling & Development*, 82, 131–138.

Haque, A. (2004). Psychology from Islamic perspective: Contributions of early Muslim scholars and challenges to contemporary Muslim psychologists. *Journal of Religion & Health*, 43, 357–377. https://doi.org/10.1007/s10943-004-4302-z.

Heelas, P., & Lock, A. (1981). *Indigenous psychologies: The anthropology of the self.* London: Academic Press.

Heidegger, M. (1962). *Being and time* (J. Macquarrie & E. Robinson, Trans.). New Haven, CT: Yale University Press.

Hewitt, M. (2012). Affective and cognitive dimensions of religious experience: Toward a conceptual/theoretical integrative perspective. *Studies in Religion*, 41(1), 33–45.

Hill, C. E., Knox, S., Thompson, B. J., Williams, E. N., Hess, S. A., & Ladany, N. (2005). Consensual qualitative research: An update. *Journal of Counseling Psychology*, 52, 196–205.

Hill, C. E., Thompson, B. J., & Williams, E. N. (1997). A guide to conducting consensual qualitative research. *The Counseling Psychologist*, 25, 517–572.

Himelhoch, S., & Njie-Carr, V. (2016). "God loves me no matter how I am": A phenomenological analysis of the religious and spiritual experiences of HIV-infected African-American women with depression. *Mental Health, Religion & Culture*, 19(2), 178–191. doi:10.1080/13674676.2016.1138934.

Ho, D. Y. F. (1988). Asian psychology. A dialogue in indigenization and beyond. In A. C. Paranjpe, D. Y. F. Ho, & R. W. Rieber (Eds.), Asian contributions to psychology (pp. 53–77). New York: Praeger.

Hood, A. B., & Johnson, R. W. (1997). *Assessment in counseling: A guide to psychological assessment procedures* (2nd ed.). Alexandria, VA: American Counseling Association.

Hood, R. W. Jr. (2000). American psychology of religion and the "Journal for the Scientific Study of Religion." *Journal for the Scientific Study of Religion*, 39(4), 531–542.

Hood, R. W. Jr. (2010). "Towards cultural psychology of religion: Principles, approaches, and applications": An appreciative response to Belzen's invitation. *Mental Health, Religion & Culture*, 13(4), 397–406.

Hood, R. W. Jr. (2013). Methodological diversity in the psychology of religion and spirituality. In K. I. Pargament (Ed.) *APA handbook of psychology, religion and spirituality, Vol. 1.: Context, theory, and research* (pp. 79–102). Washington, DC: American Psychological Association.

Hood, R. W. Jr., & Belzen, J. (2005). Research methods in the psychology of religion. In R. F. Paloutzian & C. L. Parks (Eds.), *Handbook of religion and spirituality* (pp. 62–79). New York: The Guilford Press.

Hood, R. W. Jr., Hill, P. C., & Spilka, B. (2018). *The psychology of religion: An empirical approach* (4th ed.). New York: The Guilford Press.

Hood, R. W. Jr. & Williamson, W. P. (2008). *Them that believe: The power and meaning of the Christian serpent handling tradition*. Berkely, CA: University of California Press.

Hoshmand, L. T. (1996). Cultural psychology as metatheory. *Journal of Theoretical and Philosophical Psychology*, 16, 30–48.

Hoshmand, L. T. (2005). Narratology, cultural psychology, and counseling research. *Journal of Counseling Psychology*, 52(2), 178–186.

Howard, G. (1991). Culture tales: A narrative approach to thinking, crosscultural psychology, and psychotherapy. *American Psychologist*, 46, 187–197.

Hussain, D., & Bhushan, B. (2011). Cultural factors promoting coping among Tibetan refugees: A qualitative investigation. *Mental Health, Religion & Culture*, 14(6), 575–587. Doi: 10.1080/13674676.2010.497131.

Hwang, K. K., & Huang, G. (2012). *Foundations of Chinese psychology: Confucian* social-relations. New York: Springer.

James, W. (1878). Brute and human intellect. *The Journal of Speculative Philosophy*, 12, 236-276.

James, W. (1884). What is an emotion? *Mind*, 9, 188–205.

James, W. (1983). *Essays in psychology*. Cambridge, MA: Harvard University Press.

Joshanloo, M. (2019). Cultural religiosity as the moderator of the relationship between affective experience and life satisfaction: A study in 147 countries. *Emotion*, 19(4), 629–636.

Josselson, R. (2013). *Interviewing for qualitative inquiry: A relational approach*. The Guildford Press.

Josselson, R. (2014). Introduction to qualitative psychology. *Qualitative Psychology*, 1(1), 1–3.

Josselson, R., & Lieblich, A. (Eds.). (1993). *The narrative study of lives: New approaches to traditional issues* (Vol. 1). Thousand Oaks, CA: Sage.

Kant, I. (1966). *Critique of pure reason*. Garden City, NY: Doubleday. (Original work published 1781).

Keefe, R. H., Brownstein-Evans, C., & Polmanteer, R. R. (2016). "I find peace there": How faith, church, and spirituality help mothers of colour cope with postpartum depression. *Mental Health, Religion & Culture*, 19(7), 722–733. doi:10.1080/13674676.2016.1244663.

Kemmis, S., & McTaggart, R. (2000). Participatory action research. In N. K. Denzin & Y. S. Lincoln (Eds.), *Handbook of qualitative research* (2nd ed., pp. 567–605). Thousand Oaks, CA: Sage.

Kim, D. S. (1999). The healing of *han* in Korean Pentecostalism. *Journal of Pentecostal Theology*, 15, 123–139.

Kim, H. J., & Pak, J. H. (2013). Journeys toward spiritual maturity among Korean immigrant women in midlife. *Journal of Psychology & Christianity*, 32 (1), 3–19.

Kim, K. (2006). Holy spirit movements in Korea—paternal or maternal? Reflections on the analysis of Ryu Tong-Shik (Yu Tong-Shik). *Exchange*, 35(2), 147–168.

Kim, U., Yang, K. S., & Hwang, K. K. (2006). *Indigenous and cultural psychology: Understanding people in context*. New York, NY: Springer.

Kincheloe, J. L., & McLaren, P. L. (1994). Rethinking critical theory and qualitative research. In N. K. Denzin & Y. S. Lincoln (Eds.), *Handbook of qualitative research* (pp. 138–157). Thousand Oaks, CA: Sage.

Kincheloe, J. L., & McLaren, P. L. (2000). Rethinking critical theory and qualitative research. In N. K. Denzin & Y. S. Lincoln (Eds.), *Handbook of qualitative research* (2nd ed., pp. 279–313). Thousand Oaks, CA: Sage.

Kroeber, A. L., & Kluckhohn, C. (1952). *Culture. A critical review of concepts and definitions*. Cambridge.

Kuhn, T. (1970). *The structure of scientific revolutions*. Chicago: University of Chicago Press.

Kvale, S. (1996). *InterViews: An introduction to qualitative research interviewing*. Thousand Oaks: Sage.

Lamiell, J. T. (1981). Toward an idiothetic psychology of personality. *American Psychologist*, 36(3), 276–289. https://doi.org/10.1037/0003-066X.36.3.276.

Lamiell, J. T. (2019). *Psychology's misuse of statistics and persistent dismissal of its critics*. Palgrave studies in the theory and history of psychology. Cham: Springer Nature.

Lange, C. [1885] (1922). The emotions. In E. Dunlap (Ed.), *The emotions*, (pp. 33–92). Baltimore, Md.: Williams & Wilkins.

Lawson, R. B., Graham, J. E., & Baker, K. M. (2007). *A history of psychology: Globalization, ideas, and applications*. New Jersey: Pearson.

Lazarus, R. S. (1982). Thoughts on relationship between emotion and cognition. *American Psychologist*, 37, 1019–24.

Leahey, T. H. (2000). *A history of psychology: Main currents in psychological thought*. Upper Saddle River, NJ: Prentice-Hall.

Leary, D. E. (2014). Overcoming blindness: Some historical reflections on qualitative psychology. *Qualitative Psychology*, 1(1), 17–33.

LeDoux, J. E. (1996). *The emotional brain*. New York: Simon and Schuster.

Lee, C. S. (2006). The Pentecostal face of Korean Protestantism: A critical understanding. *Asia Journal of Theology*, 20(2), 399–417.

Lewis-Williams, D. (2010). *Conceiving God: The cognitive origin and evolution of religion*. London: Thames & Hudson.

Lincoln, Y. S. & Guba, E. G. (1985). *Naturalistic Inquiry*. Newbury Park, CA: Sage Publications.

Mar, R. A., Oatley, K., Hirsh, J., Paz, J., Peterson, J. B. (2006). Bookworms versus nerds: Exposure to fiction versus non-fictions, divergent associations with social ability, and the simulation of fictional social worlds. *Journal of Research in Personality*, 40, 694–712.

Marecek, J. (2011). Numbers and interpretations: What is at stake in our ways of knowing? *Theory & Psychology*, 21(2), 220–240.

Marecek, J., Fine, M., & Kidder, L. (1997). Working between worlds: Qualitative methods and social psychology. *Journal of Social Issues*, 53, 631–644.

Markus, H. R., & Kitayama, S. (1991). Culture and the self: Implications for cognition, emotion, and motivation. *Psychological Review*, 98(2), 224–253.

McAdams, D. P. (1993). *The stories we live by: Personal myths and the making of the self*. New York: Morrow.

McAdams, D. P. (2001). The psychology of life stories. *Review of General Psychology*, 5, 100-122.

McAdams, D. P. (2006). *The redemptive self: Stories Americans live by*. New York: Oxford.

McClelland, S. I. (2017). Vulnerable Listening: Possibilities and Challenges of Doing Qualitative Research. *Qualitative Psychology*, 4(3), 338–352.

Meacham, J. (1999). Riegel, dialectics, and multiculturalism. *Human Development*, 42, 134–144.

Miller, P. J., Hengst, J. A., & Wang, S. H. (2003). Ethnographic methods: Applications from developmental cultural psychology. In P. M. Camic, J. E. Rhodes, & L. Yardley

(Eds.) *Qualitative research in psychology: Expanding perspectives in methodology and design* (pp. 219–242). Washington, DC: American Psychological Association.

Morrow, S. L. (2005). Quality and trustworthiness in qualitative research in counseling psychology. *Journal of Counseling Psychology*, 52(2), 250–260.

Ndlovu-Gatsheni, S. J. (2013). *Empire, global coloniality and African subjectivity*. New York, NY: Berghahn Books.

Nelson, K., & Fivush, R. (2004). The emergence of autobiographical memory: A social cultural developmental theory. *Psychological Review*, 111(2), 486–511.

Norris, R. S. (2005). Examining the structure and role of emotion: Contributions of neurobiology to the study of embodied religious experience. *Zygon*, 40(1), 181–200.

O'Neill, P. (2002). Tectonic change: The qualitative paradigm in psychology. *Canadian Psychology*, 43(3), 192–194.

Pak, J. H. (2006). *Korean American women: Stories of acculturation and changing selves*. New York: Routledge.

Pak, J. H. (2017). Cultural psychology of religion and qualitative inquiry. *Research in the Social Scientific Study of Religion*, 28, 163–187. doi.org/10.1163/9789004348936_009.

Pak, J. H. (2000). Towards understanding psychology of emotion, indigenous spirituality, and Christianity in Korea. In A. Dueck (ed.), *Indigenous psychologies of spirituality: In my beginning is my end* (pp. 203–225). Palgrave, Macmillan.

Paloutzian, R. F., & Park, C. L. (Eds.) (2nd ed.). (2013). *Handbook of the psychology of religion and Spirituality*. Guilford Press.

Panksepp, J. (1998). *Affective neuroscience: The foundations of human and animal emotions*. Oxford: Oxford University Press.

Pargament, K. I. (2007). *Spiritually integrated psychotherapy: Understanding and addressing the sacred*. New York, NY: Guilford Press.

Pargament, K. I., Mahoney, A., Exline, J., Jones, J., & Shafranske, E. P. (2013). Envisioning an integrative paradigm for the psychology of religion and spirituality. In K. I. Pargament, J. Exline, J. Jones, A. Mahoney, & E. Shafranske (Eds.), *APA handbooks in psychology: APA handbook of psychology, religion, and spirituality*. Vol. 1, context, theory, and research. Washington, DC: American Psychological Association.

Park, A. S. (1993). *The wounded heart of God: The Asian concept of Han and the Christian doctrine of sin*. Nashville: Abingdon Press.

Parsons, W. B., & Jonte-Pace, D. (2001). Introduction: Mapping religion and psychology. In W. B. Parsons & D. E. Jonte-Pace, Religion and Psychology: Mapping the terrain (p. 1–10). Routledge.

Patton, M. Q. (2014). (4th ed.). *Qualitative research and evaluation methods: Integrating theory and practice*. Newbury Park: Sage.

Pedersen, P. (1999). Culture-centered interventions as a fourth dimension of psychology. In P. Pedersen (Ed.), *Multiculturalism as a fourth force* (pp. 3–18). Philadelphia: Brunner/Mazel.

Polkinghorne, D. E. (1983). *Methodology for the human sciences: Systems of inquiry.* Albany, NY: State University of New York Press.

Polkinghorne, D. (1988). *Narrative knowing and the human sciences.* New York: State University of New York Press.

Polkinghorne, D. E. (2000). Psychological inquiry and the pragmatic and hermeneutic traditions. *Theory and Psychology*, 10, 453–479.

Polkinghorne, D. E. (2005). Language and meaning: Data collection in qualitative research. *Journal of Counseling Psychology*, 52, 137–145.

Ponterotto, J. G. (2002). Qualitative research methods: The fifth force in psychology. The *Counseling Psychologist*, 30, 394–406.

Ponterotto, J. G., Costa, C. I., & Werner-Lin, A. (2002). Research perspectives in cross-cultural counseling. In P. B. Pedersen, J. G. Draguns, W. J. Lonner, & J. E. Trimble (Eds.), *Counseling across cultures* (5th ed., pp. 395–420). Thousand Oaks, CA: Sage.

Porter, T. M. (1995). *Trust in Numbers: The Pursuit of Objectivity in Science and Public Life.* Princeton: Princeton University Press.

Rao, K. R., Paranjpe, A., & Dalal, A. (2008). (Eds.) *Handbook of Indian Psychology.* New Delhi: Cambridge University Press.

Ratner, C. (1997). *Cultural psychology and qualitative methodology: Theoretical and empirical considerations.* N.Y.: Plenum.

Ratner, C. (1999). Three approaches to cultural psychology: A critique. *Cultural Dynamics*, 11, 7–31.

Ratner, C. (2006). Epistemological, social, and political conundrums in social constructionism. *Forum for Qualitative Social Research*, 7, 1, article 4: http://www.qualitative-research.net/fqs-texte/1-06/06-1-4-e.htm.

Ratner, C. (2008a). *Cultural psychology, cross-cultural psychology, indigenous psychology.* New York: Nova Science Publishers, Inc.

Ratner, C. (2008b). Cultural psychology and qualitative methodology: Scientific and political considerations. *Culture and Psychology*, 14, 259–288.

Ratner, C. (2012). Macro-cultural psychology. In J. Valsiner (Ed.), *The Oxford handbook of culture and psychology* (pp. 207–237). New York: Oxford University Press, Inc.

Ratner, C., & Hui, L. (2003). Theoretical and methodological problems in cross-cultural psychology. *Journal for the Theory of Social Behavior*, 33, 67–94.

Rennie, D. L., Watson, K. D., & Monteiro, A. M. (2002). The rise of qualitative research in psychology. *Canadian Psychology*, 43, 179–189. doi:10.1037/h0086914.

Richardson, B. (2000). Recent concepts of narrative and the narratives of narrative theory. *Style*, 34, 168–176.

Ricoeur, P. (1977). *The rule of metaphor: Multidisciplinary studies of the creation of meaning in language* (R. Czerny, Trans.). Toronto, Ontario, Canada: University of Toronto Press.

Ricoeur, P. (1981). *Hermeneutics and the human sciences.* Cambridge: Cambridge University Press.

Riegel, K. F. (1975). Adult life crises: Toward a dialectic theory of development. In N. Datan & L. H. Ginsberg (Eds.), *Life-span development psychology: Normative life crisis.* New York: Academic Press.

Riegel, K. F. (1976). The dialectics of human development. *American Psychologist,* 31(10), 689-700.

Roberts, R. C. (2007). Emotions research and religious experience. In J. Corrigan (Ed.) *The Oxford handbook of religion and emotion,* (pp. 490–506). Oxford: Oxford University Press.

Rolls, E. T. (1999). *The brain and emotion.* Oxford: Oxford University Press.

Russell, J. A. (2003). Core affect and the psychological construction of emotion. *Psychological Review,* 110(1), 145–172.

Ryle, G. (1949). *The Concept of Mind.* London: Hutchinson.

Ryu, T. S. (2000). *The mineral veins of Korean theology* (Han'guk shinhak ui kwang-maek). Seoul: Tasan Kulbang.

Saldaña, J. (2013). *Fundamentals of qualitative research.* New York, NY: Oxford University Press.

Sarbin, T. R. (1986). (Ed). *Narrative psychology: The storied nature of human conduct.* New York: Praeger Publishers.

Schachter, S., & Singer, J. E. (1962). Cognitive, social, and psychological determinants of emotional state. *Psychological Review,* 69, 379–99.

Scheff, T. (2011). The catastrophe of scientism in social/behavioral science. *Contemporary Sociology,* 40(3), 264–268.

Seidman, I. E. (1991). *Interviewing as qualitative research.* New York: Teachers College Press.

Sherman, M. D., Usset, T., Voecks, C., & Harris, J. I. (2018). Roles of religion and spirituality among veterans who manage PTSD and their partners. *Psychology of Religion and Spirituality,* 10(4), 368–374. https://doi-org.fuller.idm.oclc.org/10.1037/relo000159.

Shweder, R. A. (1990). Cultural psychology: what is it? In J. W. Stigler, R. A. Shweder, & G. Herdt (Eds), *Cultural Psychology: Essays on Comparative Human Development* (pp. 1–43). Cambridge: Cambridge University Press.

Shweder, R. A. (1991). *Thinking through cultures: Expeditions in cultural psychology.* Cambridge, Mass: Harvard University Press.

Silverman, G. S., Johnson, K. A., & Cohen, A. B. (2016). To believe or not to believe, that is not the question: The complexity of Jewish beliefs about God. *Psychology of Religion and Spirituality,* 8(2), 119–130. doi:10.1037/rel0000065.

Singer, J. A. (2004). Narrative identity and meaning making across the adult lifespan. An introduction. *Journal of Personality,* 72(3), 437–459.

Sinha, D. (1997). Indigenizing psychology. In J. W. Berry, Y. H. Poortinga, & J. Pandey (Eds.), *Handbook of cross-cultural psychology* (pp. 130–169). Boston: Allyn & Bacon.

Sinha, D., & Holtzman, W. H. (Eds.). (1984). The impact of psychology on Third World development. *International Journal of Psychology*, 19, 3–192.

Smith, J. A. (1996). Beyond the divide between cognition and discourse: Using interpretive phenomenological analysis in health psychology. *Psychology & Health*, 11, 261–271.

Snook, D. W., Kleinmann, S. M., White, G., & Horgan, J. G. (2019). Conversion motifs among Muslim converts in the United States. *Psychology of Religion and Spirituality*. https://doi-org.fuller.idm.oclc.org/10.1037/rel0000276.

Stainton-Rogers, W., & Willig, C. (Eds.) (2017). *The Sage handbook of qualitative research in psychology*. Thousand Oaks, CA: Sage Publications Ltd.

Steinmetz, G. (2014). The sociology of empires, colonies, and postcolonialism. *Annual Review of Sociology*, 40, 77–103.

Straub, J. (2006). Understanding cultural differences: Relational hermeneutics and comparative analysis in cultural psychology. In J. Straub, D. Weidemann, C., Kolbl, B. Zielke (Eds.), *Pursuit of meaning: Advances in cultural and cross-cultural psychology* (pp. 163–213). New Brunswick: Transactions Publishers.

Straub, J., & Weidemann, D. (2006). Psychology, culture, and the pursuit of meaning: An introduction. In J. Straub, D. Weidemann, C. Kolbl, B. Zielke (Eds.), *Pursuit of meaning: Advances in cultural and cross-cultural psychology* (pp. 11–20). New Brunswick: Transactions Publishers.

Streib, H., & Hood, R. W. (Eds). (2015). *Semantics and psychology of spirituality: A cross-cultural analysis*. Switzerland: Springer International Publishing.

Sundararajan, L. (2015). *Understanding emotion in Chinese culture: Thinking through psychology*. New York: Springer.

Takriti, R. A., Barrett, M., & Buchanan-Barrow, E. (2006). Children's understanding of religion: Interviews with Arab-Muslim, Asian-Muslim, Christian and Hindu children aged 5–11 years. *Mental Health, Religion & Culture*, 9(1), 29–42. doi:10.1080/13674670512331335677.

Thin, N. (2018). Qualitative approaches to culture and well-being. In E. Diener, S. Oishi, & L. Tay (Eds.), *Handbook of well-being*. Salt Lake City, UT: DEF Publishers. DOI:nobascholar.com.

Ting, R. S.-K. (2016). Celebrating life and death: Resiliency among post-earthquake Tibetans' religious community. *Journal of Psychology & Theology*, 44(2), 124–132.

Valsner, J. (2014). Needed for cultural psychology: Methodology in a new key. *Culture & Psychology*, 20(1), 3–30.

Vieten, C., Scammell, S., Pilato, R., Ammondson, I., Pargament, K., & Lukoff, D. (2013). Spiritual and religious competencies for psychologists. *Psychology of Religion and Spirituality*, 5(3), 129–144.

Vygotsky, L. S. (1978). *Mind in society: the development of higher psychological processes.* (Ed. & trans. M. Cole) Cambridge, MA: Harvard University Press.

Wang, Q., & Brockmeier, J. (2002). Autobiographical remembering as cultural practice: Understanding the interplay between memory, self and culture. *Culture & Psychology*, 8(1), 45–64.

Watters, E. (2011). The wave that brought PTSD to Sri Lanka. In E. Watters (Ed.), *Crazy like us: The globalization of the American psyche* (pp. 65–126). New York, NY: Free Press.

Wertz, F. J. (2011). The qualitative revolution and psychology: Science, politics, and ethics. *The Humanistic Psychologist*, 39, 77–104. doi:10.1080/ 08873267.2011.564531.

Wertz, F. J. (2014). Qualitative inquiry in the history of psychology. *Qualitative Psychology*, 1, 4–16.

Wertz, F. J., Charmaz, K., McMullen, L., Josselson, R., Anderson, R., & McSpadden, E. (2011). *Five ways of doing qualitative analysis: Phenomenological psychology, grounded theory, discourse analysis, narrative research, and intuitive inquiry.* New York, NY: Guilford Press.

Williams, L. M., Jiang, Y., & Rector, E. (2018). How couples navigate different beliefs about god's existence: An exploratory study among Catholics and their agnostic or atheist partners. *Journal of Psychology and Christianity*, 37(4), 293–304.

Williamson, W. P., Pollio, H. R., & Jr., R. W. (2000). A Phenomenological Analysis of the Anointing among Religious Serpent Handlers. *International Journal for the Psychology of Religion*, 10(4), 221–240. doi:10.1207/s15327582ijpr1004_02.

Winkelman, M. (2004). Shamanism as the original neurotheology. *Zygon*, 39(1), 193–217.

Wittenstein, L. (1968). (3rd ed.). *Philosophical investigation.* Translated by G. E. M. Anscombe, New York: Macmillan.

Wulff, D. M. (2003) A field in crisis: Is it time to start over? In H. M. P. Roelofsma, J. M. T. Corveleyn, & J. W. van Saane (Eds.), *One hundred years of psychology of religion* (pp. 11–32). Amsterdam: VU University Press.

Wundt, W. (1921). *Elements of folk psychology*. London: Allen & Unwin.

Yang, K. S. (2012). Indigenous psychology, westernized psychology and indigenized psychology: A non-western psychologist's view. *Chang Gung Journal of Humanities and Social Sciences*, 5(1), 1–32.

Ziliak, S., & McCloskey, D. (2008). *The Cult of Statistical Significance*. Ann Arbor: University of Michigan Press.